ABERDEEN UNIVERSITY 1945–1981 REGIONAL ROLES AND NATIONAL NEEDS

AUP titles of related interest

THE STUDENT COMMUNITY AT ABERDEEN 1860–1939
R D Anderson

ABERDEEN AND THE ENLIGHTENMENT
edited by Jennifer J Carter and Joan H Pittock

WILLIAM ELPHINSTONE AND THE KINGDOM OF
SCOTLAND 1431–1514
Leslie J Macfarlane

EMIGRATION FROM NORTH-EAST SCOTLAND
Volume 1 Willing Exiles
Volume 2 Beyond the Broad Atlantic
Marjory Harper

LITERATURE OF THE NORTH
edited by David Hewitt and Michael Spiller

University of Aberdeen ROLL OF GRADUATES 1956–1970 with
Supplement 1860–1955
compiled by Louise Donald and William S MacDonald

QUINCENTENNIAL STUDIES
in the history of
THE UNIVERSITY OF ABERDEEN

ABERDEEN UNIVERSITY 1945–1981
REGIONAL ROLES AND
NATIONAL NEEDS

Edited by
John D Hargreaves with Angela Forbes

Published for the University of Aberdeen by
ABERDEEN UNIVERSITY PRESS
Member of Maxwell Macmillan Pergamon Publishing Corporation

First published 1989
Aberdeen University Press

© University of Aberdeen 1989

British Library Cataloguing in Publication Data

Aberdeen University 1945–1981: regional roles and national
    needs.—(Quincentennial studies in the history of the
    University of Aberdeen)
1. Scotland. Grampian Region. Aberdeen. Universities.
University of Aberdeen History
I. Hargreaves, John D. (John Desmond), *1924*– II. Forbes, Angela
378.412′35

ISBN 0 08 037971 0

Typeset from author-generated discs
and printed by AUP Glasgow/Aberdeen—A member of BPCC Ltd.

Foreword

In 1995 the University of Aberdeen celebrates five hundred years of continuous existence. Some eighty other European universities had been established before 1500, of which about fifty have survived to the later twentieth century, though not all of those with an uninterrupted history. At Aberdeen, King's College and University was founded in 1495, and Marischal College in 1593, the two combining to form a single university in 1860. Such a long institutional life invites close historical study, as well as celebration; but the 1980s are not an easy time for British universities, and it is therefore the more striking that in 1984 the governing body of the University of Aberdeen decided to commission a series of historical studies in honour of the quincentenary. The decision to commit funds to the project, and to give the Editorial Board such a free hand as we have had, makes the University Court's decision the braver and more honourable.

The first study in our Quincentennial series appeared in 1988. It was a short monograph, of the type we plan to multiply before 1995—R D Anderson, *The Student Community at Aberdeen 1860–1939*. This second contribution to the series is of a different sort, being the edited version of papers delivered at public seminars held at the university early in 1989. It was the aim of the seminars both to capture memories, and to stimulate analysis of the university's history between 1945 and 1981, a period of unprecedented growth and change. The period opened with the university cautiously but sensibly planning its post-war regeneration. It closed with Aberdeen taking more than its expected share in the funding cuts imposed on all British universities by the University Grants Committee. Those cuts were interpreted as critical of the university's record, especially in research: the low research-rating given by the UGC to Aberdeen's long-prized Medical School came as a particular shock to local opinion. Many members of the university began to look more critically at the years before 1981, either to attack or to defend our record. This was not the intention of the seminars. Rather we wished to understand and explain what had happened in the thirty-six years before 1981. In that time the university expanded from about 1000 to over 6000 students. Many changes accompanied that growth, both internal changes and, more important, changes in the whole climate within which universities lived. From its nature, this is not a heavily-researched, and certainly not a definitive study, but the ideas which were put forward at the seminars, and the problems which emerged from them about approaching the recent history of the university within its regional and national context, seemed interesting enough to warrant publication.

Chapters 1 to 7 represent revised versions of the introductory papers prepared for the seminars. The valuable presentations made by our invited commentators, and some of the spontaneous contributions from members of the audience, appear in this volume in three different forms. Some points have been taken into account during revision of the introductory papers; direct acknowledgement is rarely possible, but the editors wish to record their general gratitude to all who took part in the discussions. Those prepared contributions which drew heavily on personal experience and memory, and so have the character of primary evidence, are printed as appendices to the relevant chapters. Summaries of the remaining invited commentaries, and of some of the most important contributions from the floor, have been incorporated, with formal attribution, in John Hargreaves' concluding chapter of 'Summaries and Signposts'. We hope that this publication may stimulate the contribution of further memoirs to the university's archives.

The Editorial Board is most grateful to Sir Kenneth Alexander, Chancellor of the University, whose own contribution to the seminars' success was striking. Particular thanks are due to two contributors who have no direct connection with the university but gave generously of their time and talent—Professor John Cannon and Mr Edward Cunningham. Our special thanks go also to Mr Colin MacLean, Managing Director of Aberdeen University Press, not only as our ever-helpful publisher, but on account of his own significant contribution to the seminars. Producing this volume quickly would not have been possible without the skilled, patient and expert help of the Faculty Secretariat, and we are most grateful to Mrs Jenny Albiston, Mrs Lorna Cardno and Mrs Gill Silver. Professor John Hargreaves devised and directed the seminars, and his fellow-members of the Editorial Board thank him warmly for carrying through a difficult assignment with much grace. He was assisted, especially in recording the sessions, by Miss Angela Forbes, to whom likewise the Editorial Board offers warm thanks.

JENNIFER CARTER
General Editor

Contents

Authors and Commentators

Sir Kenneth Alexander, Chancellor of the University, was a lecturer in political economy, 1957–62

N R D Begg has been Secretary to the university since 1988

John Cannon is professor of history at the University of Newcastle-upon-Tyne. He was a member of the University Grants Committee, 1983–89, and its vice-chairman from 1986

Jennifer Carter, senior lecturer in history, is General Editor of the Quincentennial Studies in the History of the University of Aberdeen

Edward Cunningham is Director (Planning and Projects) of the Scottish Development Agency

Angela Forbes is a research student in the history department

Sandra Galbraith is a research assistant in economics

Max Gaskin was professor of political economy, 1965–85

Charles Gimingham, who first joined the university staff in 1945, was professor of botany, 1969–89

John Hargreaves was professor of history, 1962–85

I G C Hutchison, an Aberdeen graduate, is lecturer in history at the University of Stirling

Alex Kemp has been professor of economics since 1983

Donald MacKinnon was professor of moral philosophy at Aberdeen, 1947–60

Colin McLaren is Keeper of Manuscripts and University Archivist

Colin MacLean is Managing Director of Aberdeen University Press

Michael Meston, professor of private law since 1971, was vice-principal 1979–82

John Nisbet was professor of education, 1963–89

Willis Pickard, editor of *The Times Educational Supplement* (*Scotland*), was elected Rector of the University in 1987

John Raeburn was professor of agriculture, 1959–78

Gerard Rochford was professor of social work, 1978–89

John Sewel is dean of the faculty of economic and social science

T B Skinner was Secretary to the university, 1968–84

David Strachan, president of the SRC 1974–75, is Managing Director, Tern Television

Roy Weir has been professor of community medicine since 1969

Introduction

SIR KENNETH ALEXANDER

The writing of recent history must be one of the most challenging tasks facing historians, and even more challenging if the historians who take up this challenge were themselves part of the history they seek to set out and comment upon. This book is the product of such a difficult process. However I do not think it could have been better done, and probably it could not have been done at all if this method had not been adopted.

The method was to invite papers from academics and others, most of whom had had a direct association with the university during the 1945–81 period. These papers were then presented to a series of seminars attended by a wider group, most of whom had also been involved with the university during that period. The seminar provided an opportunity for questions to be asked, for additional information to be offered, and for alternative versions and explanations of particular aspects of the story to be advanced. The seminars were recorded, the original papers revised where appropriate, and the whole used by John Hargreaves and Angela Forbes in an excellent chapter of 'Summaries and Signposts'. In the preparation of this volume it has fallen to John Hargreaves in particular to operate on the principle so clearly set out by J R Lucas, interestingly based on his university experience:

> History is not just biography, and an incident that looms large in one man's experience may seem quite different and much less significant to a dispassionate observer.[1]

The preparation of most papers required the careful sifting of relevant documentation, not always as readily available or as detailed and explicit as historians might wish. Universities have (or perhaps had, given the new managerial broom of recent years) a labyrinthine network of hier-archically-structured committees, and it would be reasonable to expect that historical studies would be greatly helped by the minutes of these committees. But here I must make a personal confession. In the interests

1

of clearly recording decisions and avoiding wasting time on correcting minutes of the individual contributions of committee members I have frequently told minute-takers (at Stirling University): 'Keep them brief. You are not writing the history of the University'. My association with this exercise has led me to wonder whether this was false economy. Inevitably, of course, the extant paper-work cannot reflect fully the interests and opinions which influenced decision-taking. Additionally the period being reviewed saw a very considerable increase in the openness of decision-taking to the various sectional interests within universities. As a consequence it seems likely that what we know about the sixties and seventies is fuller and more accurate than what we know about the forties and fifties.

Another aspect of the writing of history is the extent to which it is proper to use contemporary values in the judgement of past behaviour. Although it might be thought that over as short a period as forty years no change in attitudes or values was likely to be significant enough to make this an important issue, I doubt whether this is the case. Attitudes to expansion, to optimum size, to 'relevance', and indeed to the role of universities in society, have changed substantially over this particular short period. The authors have, in my view quite rightly, tried to explain decision-taking in the context of the time at which the particular choice had to be made, but have not hesitated to apply some hindsight in their assessment of such decisions. The value of the book is not simply to record but is also to ask questions about alternatives which may have been open to the university at the time. It is to the credit of the authors and those who attended the seminars that despite the particularly difficult circumstances of the University of Aberdeen at the present time the allocation of 'blame' has not been an objective of the exercise. To a properly cautious empiricism has been added an even more careful consideration of alternatives and judging of choices, all helped by a collective rather than an individualistic approach to the editing process.

To criticise the book for largely ignoring the implications (other than in relation to government and the University Grants Committee) of the broader sweep of university development and change in Scotland and the United Kingdom would be to criticise the authors for holding firm to their narrower objective—to record some forty years in the history of one university. It is of great importance that the role of the universities in the nation's histories—economic, social, scientific and cultural—be examined and assessed by objective historians, and this broader task will be greatly assisted by this and similar studies.

The greatest interest in the book will be amongst graduates and academics who have a direct association with the university. Because of the specially strong regional links which the university has built up over the centuries there are also aspects of this history which will be of great interest to others living in the north of Scotland. As a lecturer at the university in the 1950s I have most pleasant memories of the response we had when we took 'University Weeks' to Orkney, Shetland and the Western Isles, and on other extra-mural forays throughout the north.

Readers will be, as I am, indebted to the authors and editors for sharpening our memories and perceptions of the recent past of the university, and changing some of these in a most interesting way. This history is an appropriate and indeed splendid precursor to the University of Aberdeen's Quincentenary celebrations which we look forward to in 1995.

Chapter 1

Academic Strategies of Expansion

JOHN HARGREAVES

Before and immediately after the Second World War Aberdeen ranked eleventh in size among the British universities, just above Bristol. But student numbers had long been declining from their 1921 peak of 1,600; in 1944 there were only 960 full-time undergraduates, plus twelve research students. Medicine, with 397 undergraduates, remained the largest faculty, directed as a largely autonomous entity by the redoubtable David Campbell, dean from 1932 until 1959. National Service had reduced the faculty of arts by almost a quarter from its pre-war level, to 321, but science had increased to a record 225. Law had only eight students and divinity (with its six professors) nine, while 58 per cent of students had home addresses within thirty miles of Aberdeen. The academic staff, including 31 persons absent on war service and 14 temporary appointments, numbered 121: 42 assistants, 44 lecturers, 4 readers and 31 professors. All but seven of the professors were Scots-born and had attended Scottish universities, although only six were graduates of Aberdeen. At least half had home addresses in Old Aberdeen; Senatus meetings, usually attended by under twenty members, were gatherings of colleagues who knew (but did not necessarily like) each other well. The university office was run by the formidable Colonel Butchart at a cost of under £10,000, setting a hard standard of economical administration for all British universities.

Depleted by war though the university might be, its post-war plan, submitted to the UGC in March 1944, seems imaginative and well-considered. It proposed to specialise in 'the Biological Sciences—Agriculture, Forestry, and Marine Biology—without neglecting those other branches of science on which their development to a large extent depends'. Application of these studies in north-east Scotland might, it was hoped, 'bring to these branches of Scottish Industry assistance not incomparable to that which Scottish Universities gave to other industries at the time of the Industrial Revolution by their studies in Chemistry and Physics'. Aberdeen's qualifications for this role were emphasised by reference to plans for co-operation with the research institutes: Boyd Orr had retained the directorship of the Rowett on becoming professor of agriculture, and Professor Alister Hardy was collaborating with the two Torry research stations. To sustain this expansion the university planned to remove the science departments—in the first instance, chemistry—from Marischal to 'a large building to be erected on a site already in the possession of the University'. It was shortly decided that this should be in Old Aberdeen; some medics wanted it to be at Foresterhill, where anatomy and physiology were destined to occupy 'a new wing'. More generally, there was emphasis on improving tutorial instruction and advice for undergraduates, on new teaching methods (including more use of documents and provision of a cinematograph), and on encouraging research by all members of staff. This emphasis on teaching in an atmosphere of research is perhaps the most consistent feature of academic planning throughout the period. A sum of £6,400 was requested to extend the library stacks; the university declared its intention to establish halls of residence for women and men students, once the capital cost came down to the pre-war figure of £668 per head.

These modest and practical proposals, based on assessments of regional needs as well as of the strengths of the university's staff at that moment, were substantially approved, and from 1944 public money began to flow. At the conference of Scottish Courts in May 1945 Sir Hector Hetherington hinted that increased dependence on Treasury funds might have implications for university autonomy; but there was no alternative if universities were to do what the post-war public clearly expected of them. By 1948 student numbers reached a temporary peak of 2,148. There were already signs that this might not satisfy the UGC; but at this stage there was little desire to go further. On 1 June 1946 Principal Fyfe, on the advice of the faculties, declared that the 'optimum maximum' figure was 2,500 'and that any number above that would entirely alter the nature of the University'.

For some years this remained a theoretical issue. After the rush of ex-service students Aberdeen's numbers fell back more strongly than in UK universities generally; despite a growing intake from overseas from the mid 1950s they did not again reach their 1948 level until 1959–60 (whereas the UK total did so in 1955–6). But the inter-faculty balance had changed. Medicine, after an uncomfortable expansion to around 550 to accommodate ex-service demand, settled back at its pre-war figure of 430; by 1961–2 this represented just over 20 per cent of the undergraduate body, as compared to 40 per cent pre-war. Arts had increased its share from 39 per cent to 46 per cent; but the most spectacular increase was in science, where the 626 undergraduates of 1961–2 constituted 30 per cent, compared to 13.4 per cent in 1938–9. Around one-fifth of the scientists were engineers (and the lengthy debate about relationships with Robert Gordon's had begun); forestry maintained a steady total between 40 and 60; the planned expansion in agriculture proved harder to sustain, and in 1960–1 there were only 32 undergraduates, compared to the 1948 peak of 100. Science also led the gradual growth of the university's population of research students.

The directions of scientific growth more or less followed the lines proposed in 1944. The department of soil science opened in 1947, and the creation of the chair of biochemistry in the same year was a natural development from existing commitments. In 1950 ICI supported a new lectureship in 'History and Philosophy of Scientific Research'. But until the completion of the Chemistry Building and the arrival of the first electron microscope in 1952, major innovations, as well as student numbers, were doubtless constrained by the accommodation available in Marischal.

In arts new subjects were introduced more eclectically. Biblical study, for which a lectureship was established in 1945, and music (the organist having been appointed to a part-time lectureship in 1942) became graduating courses. There was much zeal for foreign languages. From 1946 the Swedish government supported the teaching of their language, beginning a link on which Principal Taylor was particularly keen; and in 1948, on a suggestion from the SRC, Count Neri Cappone was appointed to teach Italian for £4 a week and free lunches. Established lectureships in both subjects followed in 1950, though a comparable attempt to introduce Magyar came to nothing. The university's response to the Scarborough Committee, a somewhat half-hearted bid for 'the group of languages Greek, Turkish, Albanian and Roumanian' resulted in the appointment of Hector Thomson to teach modern Greek. Social sciences at first developed less rapidly; the university's bid to the Clapham Committee of 1947, emphasising research in economic history, was not fully accepted, but in 1948 we were enabled to found a lectureship in international relations, a discipline not yet widely recognised in the UK. Professor Black's reconstruction of the history syllabus brought, among other things, new lectureships in political theory and in Scottish history. The establishment of the chair of jurisprudence in 1950, as a first stage in Principal Taylor's design for a genuine faculty of law, further broadened the menu available to students in arts.

During the 1950s the expansionist euphoria abated, though new appointments continued to be made in existing departments. Taylor told the UGC in 1951 that demand from northern Scotland seemed to have stabilised, and that, though additional students from the south or overseas would be acceptable in arts, law and divinity, the university had 'entered a period of consolidation, and indeed of reduction'. Many academics seem to have welcomed the respite as an opportunity to improve tutorial provision (including, in some departments, reading parties at The Burn), provide pastoral advice to students through the new Regent scheme, and think about future directions of research.

Speaking as one who joined the staff during this period, it is my impression that a good deal was achieved in this steady-state university. It is difficult (and not required by my brief) to assess research, but at this time quality was certainly not measurable by the amount of external funding attracted. Although many branches of science did now require substantial investment in expensive equipment, not all did so. It was not so long since Sir George Paget Thomson had laid the foundations for his Nobel prize in the laboratories of Marischal College, the high quality of technical assistance compensating for any shortcomings in equipment. Sir Dugald Baird's pioneering research in obstetrics did not require the establishment of a directly funded MRC unit until 1955. In the natural sciences, though Hardy and Boyd Orr had moved on, the proximity of the research institutes remained a great stimulus. And many teachers in the faculty of arts were able to produce quite creditable results with support which the university could provide from its own resources—the modest travel grants supported by Carnegie funds, and the expanding library.

However the research achievements of this period might be assessed by modern UGC criteria, they had invigorating effects on academic life as a whole. This was a period when scholars in different disciplines talked to one another about the sort of problems raised in Bruce Truscot's *Redbrick University* (1943), in the Harvard report on *General Education in a Free Society* (1946), in Walter Moberley's *The Crisis in the University* (1949). There were genuine exchanges among scholars in Dr Wightman's seminars on the history and philosophy of science, the AUT's Inter-Faculty Group, and in less formal meetings in that little senior common room at King's which Professor MacKinnon was particularly anxious to develop. Inter-disciplinary contacts extended to undergraduate teaching, though not always with official support; when three young scholars later to become eminent offered a joint seminar on international trade, Colonel Butchart suggested that they should charge additional fees. Possibly some elements in the Scottish university tradition are more Thatcherite than we like to think!

With around 1,700 students Aberdeen remained relatively small, over-taken in the numbers league by Bristol and Sheffield, and still deeply rooted in northern Scotland (which provided more than three-quarters of its students). In 1962, 27 of the 40 professors were Scottish-born, and 30 held degrees from Scottish universities—though these proportions were smaller among the growing number of non-professorial teachers of arts and sciences. Principal Sir Thomas Taylor had clear views of Aberdeen as a distinctively Scottish university, which 'should look to Europe at least as much as to England'.[1] Taylor was in most respects a conservative academic, sometimes criticised for applying his own strict moral standards too narrowly to university affairs—although, after due consideration, he was willing to support such radical innovations as co-educational residence, unknown in Scotland (except for medical students with clinical responsibilities) until Crombie Hall opened in 1960. But though Taylor had once been a Labour candidate, his image of Scotland and its relation to Europe was shaped less by democratic impulses deriving from the eighteenth-century Enlightenment than by older institutions, the Law and the Kirk. His graduation addresses increasingly warned against dangers of 'hyper-trophied intellectualism', of over-enthusiastic applications of science, still more of social science. He was not a natural expansionist. Access to the 'commonwealth of learning' Taylor regarded as a privilege to be earned, though he always insisted that opportunities to do so should be made widely accessible.

The university's initial plans for the quinquennium 1957–62 were still influenced by this meritocratic elitism; they envisaged increasing student numbers to 2,250, only just above the post-war peak, and still drawn mainly from the traditional catchment area. In science, it was assumed that a firm limit was set by accommodation for the freshman class in natural philosophy, which reconstruction in Marischal College was raising from 160 to 200. Nevertheless the Senatus managed to justify a substantial shopping list: new chairs in archaeology, Russian, history of art and, more ambitiously, in geophysics; new lectureships in existing departments; £100,000 worth of scientific equipment; an archivist and a curator for the museum. But on 25 April 1956 a UGC visitation made clear that they regarded the numerical targets as over-modest; they expected Aberdeen to accept more students from outside the traditional area, to prepare for a higher proportion of scientists, and to consider introducing more courses of postgraduate instruction. Their implicit offer could hardly be refused. When the visitors met the Senatus, Professor R V Jones, already convinced that the national need for scientists called for a doubling of students by recruitment beyond the region, stated that:

> the heads of Science departments would generally like to expand, and he for one felt that we had too few students in relation to the staff and equipment available and were working below the economic figure in this respect.

The key to expansion in science now seemed to be improved accommodation and extra staff in natural philosophy, mathematics and chemistry; student numbers in agriculture and forestry now seemed static, and the emphasis on applied biological sciences had disappeared from undergraduate, though not from research, planning. The university's final submission included a 'Note on Long-term Policy' indicating that, if further expansion was needed after 1962, a new natural philosophy building must be speedily planned, while a science intake above 300 would require yet more accommodation for second- and third-year chemistry classes.

Taylor now recognised, possibly with regret, that expansion would have to accelerate. In June 1957, six years before the Robbins Report, the architect Robert Mathew was commissioned to advise on the long-term development of Old Aberdeen, which the principal regarded as the spiritual as well as the physical heart of the university. Meanwhile many colleagues were responding eagerly to expansionist pressures. When science applications rose dramatically in 1957 the Senatus called for an accelerated building programme, so that admissions might reach 240 by 1960. But when 1960 came this target was already obsolete; the UGC now suggested planning for intakes rising to 600 in science and 400 in arts, leading to totals of 4,000 undergraduates and 500 postgraduates by 1970. The Court, emphasising that the UGC would need to fund residences to accommodate some 1,750 students from beyond the traditional area, commented that 'the character of the University would be fundamentally changed'. But, noting the academic advantages which fully-funded expansion on this scale might bring, it proceeded to quantify the capital costs; and it also responded positively next year when the UGC suggested raising the medical intake from 80 to 100.

So during Taylor's last years changing perceptions of national needs, allied to growing consciousness of new academic frontiers which might be opened with increased resources, already outweighed the attractions of remaining a compact university thirled to the needs of northern Scotland. Plans for the campus that we see around us were already well advanced. Since Taylor's talents and interests did not lie in the administration of building programmes, in September 1960 he demitted the convenership of the Edilis committee to Professor Edward Wright, who next year also became our first vice-principal. When Taylor died in July 1962 Wright was thus an obvious candidate to succeed him, and the execution of the planned expansion took place under his leadership.

During the 1960s the pace continued to accelerate. In November 1963, following the acceptance of the Robbins Report, Senatus and Court agreed to a UGC request to advance the 4,500 target to 1967–8; but, as they pointed out, to increase admissions so rapidly would create a momentum to carry the total towards 6,000 by 1970. This phase of expansion was completed more or less according to plan; a total of 6,079 (including 292 B Ed students taught largely in the College of Education) was reached in 1970–1, though with a lower proportion of science students than originally intended. The academic opportunities opened by the funding provided for this were appreciated in many departments, and enthusiasm for expansion grew. In October 1965 the university proposed that in the next quin-quennium 'expansion should not stop at 5,500, but should go on to 8,000 or 10,000 by some such date as 1980', and the UGC welcomed this. After discussions in 1969–70 they proposed a target of 8,180 (later reduced by 200 science places) by 1976–7; and on 7 October 1970 the Senate accepted this by a majority of 46 to 19.

There were various reasons to hesitate before accepting a second decade of hectic expansion. Traditionalists who still shared Taylor's fears about diluting Aberdeen's traditional role in providing a sound liberal education for the academic elite of northern Scotland were now powerfully reinforced by Professor R V Jones. As early as 1964 Jones expressed fears that the university was not responding adequately to the challenges of the times, and saw his hopes of combining increased numbers with increasing scientific excellence jeopardised by 'an academic drain to the south east' of able students and distinguished staff.[2] Others who perceived no fall in standards and remained eager to share in the national expansion of uni-versity education had practical reservations, notably about how the additional students could be economically housed in a city now strongly affected by the oil boom. In 1972 Principal Wright himself feared that 'the last 500 of the total expansion, and perhaps the last 1,000, add dis-astrously and unnecessarily to the dangers and difficulties of the whole exercise'. But the majority of the Senate, fearing the consequences of opting out of the national trend, were very willing to co-operate, stipu-lating only that the UGC should provide the heavy funding needed for staff and student housing as well as for academic buildings; should maintain staff-student ratios; and should require no dilution of entrance standards.

Was it prudent to expect these conditions to be met? Since 1968 there had been signs that the government was becoming anxious about the costs of implementing Robbins' proposals; in 1969 Shirley Williams invited the universities to consider thirteen suggestions for improving cost-efficiency, without receiving great encouragement from the responses of the uni-versities or the CVCP. But her successor at the DES does not appear to have applied strong financial restraint, and the UGC began to press for a third phase of expansion in the late 1970s. In March 1973 they tentatively suggested a figure of 10,000 to 11,000 for 1981–2; when the Senatus conditionally accepted the lower figure the UGC asked for 10,500, with a strong warning of displeasure if this was not accepted. (Let us recall that our actual numbers continued to fluctuate around 5,800 through the 1970s and that 6,000 was not reached again until 1983.) But then the tide began to turn. As early as January 1974 the UGC began to require economies; the system of quinquennial planning was abandoned; the 1981 target was reduced to 8,600 and eventually to 6,000.

Why, the beleaguered academics of the 1980s may ask, did the UGC require Aberdeen to take such a disproportionate—and, as it proved, unrealistic—share of the national expansion?[3] One possible reason may have been that the university already possessed land in the Aulton available for development in accordance with Mathew's plan. In 1965, when the UGC undertook a nation-wide survey of available sites, they sagely observed that 'the cost of land required for future expansion is a considerable factor in drawing up a long-term strategy of university expansion. But it is, of course, only one of the factors involved'.[4] Figures of expenditure during the following quinquennium suggest that it was in fact a marginal one. In the five years from 1967 to 1972 'Purchase of sites and properties' cost 5 per cent of the amount spent on 'Building Works' in British universities; for Aberdeen the proportion was 1.4 per cent. This was certainly a significant economy, but it would be surprising if it was sufficient to determine 'long-term strategy', especially since heavy investment in residence was necessary in Aberdeen.[5] Another possible reason was UGC approval of the academic environment created during the 1950s, with what was at least a respectable record in research and scholarship balanced by the strong commitment to the teaching and guidance of undergraduates. One former member tells me that Aberdeen was regarded as 'a very special place'. And possibly there was a preference to see the main burden of expansion carried by mature institutions rather than the new and more experimental 'plate-glass universities' of the 1960s, where young and relatively inexperienced academics were in positions of leadership.

For the university, the inducements to expand were certainly attractive; but changes in official attitudes since 1981 call into question the wisdom of accepting a second decade of expansion which many privately thought unrealistic. Warnings which Jones expressed to the Senatus on 7 October 1970 about the loss of freedom in face of central planning have gained in retrospective weight. But the general consensus did not support Jones's view that more had meant worse: that the expansion of the 1960s lowered standards of teaching and research, and threatened our sense of academic community. Most departments had welcomed increases in staff, library and laboratory resources, research funding, which enabled them to extend their coverage and keep pace with expanding disciplinary frontiers—all to evident public approval. There was a very different climate before the cultural revolution; politicians and pundits agreed—sometimes a bit uncritically, perhaps—that expanding higher education was a thoroughly sound national investment. Perhaps this made some of us a bit complacent—or triumphalist, to recall the prevailing jargon. But while the universities remained popular, Hetherington's warning of 1945 about government control seemed alarmist; the prudent course was to retain the confidence of our paymaster. Most university teachers assumed that state funding provided the only viable basis for academic growth, and that an enlightened UGC, supported by public opinion, would provide adequate protection against governmental interference or governmental incompetence. It did not seem wise to disappoint the UGC, nor even to suggest that they might occasionally be unrealistic.

Accepting the principle of expansion does not of course imply that its strategy was well considered or well managed. Given the speed at which student numbers were expected to grow, the tendency of the Court was to direct the new resources to those departments where the staff-student ratio was deteriorating. Since it seemed important to allow students great freedom of choice—among honours courses as well as within the traditional ordinary degrees—growth was affected by changes in student demand which were not always stable or predictable. The speed of the operation left little time to devise a new strategy for the university as a whole, and the traditional division of functions between Court and Senatus did not facilitate the involvement of the Senatus in such an operation. Nor perhaps was enough time given to looking at the university's responsibilities for continuing education in the wider community.

Some of those absorbed in planning undergraduate expansion may have seen the growth of the North Sea oil industry after 1969 as complicating the problem of student accommodation rather than as opening new frontiers of academic opportunity. But many criticisms of the university's record in this direction are too sweeping. Certainly the initiative in the field of off-shore engineering was allowed to pass elsewhere; the restraints on independent development which the UGC had applied since the 1950s may have had some effect here. But there were significant developments in petroleum geology (with a chair in 1973, and an M Sc course in exploration and production), in off-shore medicine, and in economics and other social sciences. If there was perhaps too little attempt to involve industry directly in the planning and financing of these developments, too easy an assumption that research should be publicly financed, this may reflect a belief that research work should not be too dependent on those whose financial interests might be affected by its results.

On the whole I do not think that Aberdeen University need be too apologetic about its record. It responded energetically to new demands for professional education. In law, demand from the more career-minded students of the 1970s produced the most spectacular expansion of any faculty, together with a greater diversification of syllabus than is apparent from Table V. The faculty of medicine met successive increases in student numbers required by the UGC (in the process extending its teaching to Inverness); and during the 1960s it carried through the major reconstruction of curriculum suggested by the General Medical Council, involving a course shortened to five years, much larger components of scientific education, and a consequent raising of entrance qualifications. As Roy Weir shows, these developments were combined with particularly strong commitments to improving public health care with the NHS, and it cannot have been easy to balance teaching and clinical responsibilities against needs for research. The outstanding success was that of Sir Dugald Baird, whose earlier experience in Glasgow had convinced him that to improve the conditions of childbirth it was essential to study environmental influences upon the health of the family. Recruiting Angus Thomson, trained to study human nutrition by Boyd Orr, Baird built up the unique multi-disciplinary research team which became the Obstetric Medicine Research Unit of the MRC. Sadly the structures which Baird had created could not be maintained under his successor, though the Medical Sociology Research Unit remained in Aberdeen until 1984.

In science, though the growth in undergraduate numbers did not meet the expectations of 1963, the tendency seems to have been to reinforce the traditional core departments, while establishing new ones on growing frontiers of biological research. There seems to have been some movement from physical towards natural sciences. Agriculture and forestry resumed the growth foreseen in 1945, helped by substantial intakes from overseas; partnership between the *agros* and the *agris* was consolidated in the new School of Agriculture, while forestry survived an early UGC exercise in rationalisation in 1968. Independent development in engineering continued to be constrained by UGC advice. Let us add that the faculty of science continued to pioneer the development of taught postgraduate courses, and to carry the lion's share of a graduate student body enlarged from thirty or so in the post-war years to 578 in 1970–71 and 773 in 1980–81.

The faculty of arts decided in the early 1960s to undertake a significant strengthening and diversification of its provision for study of the social sciences, as well as two subjects which were to offer increasing vocational opportunities: computing and accountancy. Equally deliberately, it repeatedly resolved that it wished these new developments to take place within a large united faculty, where students could enjoy very great flexibility in their choice of courses. With the same intention of enriching the menu available to students, the faculty continued its earlier practice of adding new subjects in the humanities rather freely to its shopping lists. Unfortunately, many of these, however distinguished their teaching, have not proved sustainable under the new doctrine that academic study can only be carried on in large organisational units; of the fifteen departments established in the faculty since 1945, only politics and international relations, sociology, computing, accountancy and history of art now seem likely to survive. I do not think this need imply that it was wrong to take such initiatives when we were being urged to plan for a university of 10,500 students.

But I must beware the temptation to go beyond description of the university's strategies of expansion into attempts to justify its record. Whatever the errors and weaknesses of structure, the guiding considerations of Aberdeen's policy after 1945 were, I suggest: first, a willingness, turning perhaps too readily to eagerness, to collaborate with the UGC in the extension of national provision for university education in the UK, subject to some continuing priority for the educational needs of northern Scotland; and second, a strong commitment to improve the levels of tutorial instruction, personal guidance, and academic opportunity and choice provided for this growing undergraduate body.

Although postgraduate education and research developed even more spectacularly than undergraduate numbers, they were usually seen as symbiotic extensions of the work of teaching departments, or as partnerships with the neighbouring research institutes, rather than subjects for major autonomous initiatives. Research activities by individual teachers were given greater priority than the creation of free-standing, big-spending, research centres which might have attracted more outside contracts. I leave for discussion the question of what may have been sacrificed by the choice of these priorities, whether in the context of the painful reorientations of the 1980s or in the longer perspective of our first five hundred years.

Commentary to Chapter 1

Memories of Aberdeen, 1947–60

DONALD M MacKINNON

In the one year in which I served as regius professor of moral philosophy under Sir William Hamilton Fyfe (1947–8) an important development took place, namely the establishment of a lectureship in international relations. The first lecturer (Saul Rose) took up his duties in October 1948, and he remarked on the excellent provision of books in the field in King's College Library. This provision owed much to the prescience of that good servant of the university, Professor Alexander Stewart Ferguson (regius professor of logic, 1927–53). Ferguson's curatorship of the library, although his policies were bitterly resented by conservatives, had marked a watershed in its development, and generations of arts students have reason to bless his name for what he did to secure their base of study.

Fyfe had also secured the UGC's agreement to the most generous grants provided for any university in the UK for travel by teaching members of staff to take part in the meetings of learned societies. He rightly argued, and convinced the committee, that such provision was essential if a university as far north as Aberdeen was to continue widely to attract new staff. It was in the immediate post-war years that the numbers of lecturers greatly increased both absolutely and proportionately to other categories of teachers, making the provision that Fyfe secured vital to any sort of growth.

Thomas Murray Taylor, QC, succeeded Sir William Hamilton Fyfe in 1948. While Professor Hargreaves emphasised Taylor's conservatism, it was not for nothing that he had been a Labour man in his earlier years and that his time at the Bar had included a period as Advocate Depute to Craigie Aitchison, one of the first Lord Advocates to be appointed by a Labour administration. Further the political style of the conservatism of his later years was gleaned more from the close study of Edmund Burke than from the sort of instruction Alderman Roberts gave to the adolescent

Margaret Hilda! Again his churchmanship was indeed traditional; but he was an ardent oecumenist, and an early advocate of the ordination of women to the full ministry, eager to see women preachers invited to the King's College Chapel pulpit many years before they were even admitted to the eldership of the Church of Scotland. Again, while deeply rooted in the traditions of the Scottish Reformation, it is worth remarking that in the second year of his principalship the leading Anglo-Catholic liturgical scholar and controversialist, Dom Gregory Dix OSB, was welcomed to the pulpit at King's, and he was only one of many spokesmen of attitudes very far from Tom Taylor's own who were welcomed there.

Again, where university development was concerned, Taylor's unflinchingly Scottish commitment, shown in his support for the Scottish Covenant movement of the 1950s, led him to value greatly the characteristic ethos of a Scottish university. Thus he was always aware of the regional significance of Aberdeen University's educational and cultural role, sensitive to the strengths of the all-Scottish Ordinary degree, and inclined to be critical of the proliferation of Honours groups. Hence his attitude towards expansion when it first showed above the horizon in the later 1950s. He was finally converted to its necessity largely by the arguments of the Secretary, W S Angus, who saw expansion as the only alternative to the university's decline to the status of a liberal arts college. Taylor was a classicist, who would surely have fought to the point of resignation the recent lamentable decision by the university (pressed no-doubt by the UGC) to abandon Classics. (It is legitimate to regret that no one with Taylor's oratorical skill, not least in invective, was available to indict unsparingly this retrograde step. What is permitted to remain and grow at St David's University College, Lampeter, must disappear from Elphinstone's foundation a few years before its fifth centenary!) Yet Taylor cared greatly for the sciences, and it is impressive to note that one Gifford Lecturer of the fifties—Professor Michael Polanyi FRS—dedicated his lectures, published in 1958 under the title *Personal Knowledge*, to Sir Thomas and Lady Taylor. He disdained what he saw as slick and easy, and was always aware of fundamental moral distinctions, and imperatives. His integrity led him to speak out in 1960 against sudden contractions of government aid to universities, and the resultant damage to Aberdeen town-gown relations through cancellation of contracts, to a representative of the government concerned in a way that Sir Herbert Butterfield, then vice-chancellor of Cambridge University, who was present, found unforgettable.

It was Taylor's sense of the university as a community located geographically in north-east Scotland, and beholden to its people, that led him to hesitate at the prospect of the kind of expansion he saw as inevitable in his last years. He loved to emphasise the position of the Scottish professor as holder of a *munus publicum*. Yet he was a man of compassion, not simply an austere traditionalist. Thus when a member of the teaching staff of the university took his own life in the late autumn of 1959, from Taylor's words spoken to me, it was clear that he believed that the university as a community had failed this man. His death advertised a defect in our common life.

It would be easy to criticise the university during the years in which I knew it (1947–60) for a certain provincial cosiness born in part of its remoteness, but fostered by the concentration of its energies on its teaching role. But there were some very distinguished professors; I have mentioned Alec Ferguson; but there were also, for example, Dugald Baird among the medical clinicians; R V Jones (to whom the UK owed so much between 1939 and 1945) in the chair that had been J Clerk Maxwell's (and more recently that of Sir George Paget Thomson, whose Nobel Prize was earned by work done in Aberdeen, and was shared with the technician who had helped in the laboratory); W S Watt, successor to Sir Peter Noble, when the latter moved to the Principalship of King's College, London, a quite outstanding Latinist. There were also important innovations: Italian, Scandinavian studies (for which Aberdeen was geographically ideal), history and philosophy of science.

There were important developments in the faculty of law following the appointment of the late Professor Sir Thomas Broun Smith FBA to succeed Taylor in 1948. On becoming principal Taylor was quick to promote the appointment of a professor of jurisprudence, seeing the need to establish this key subject at the professorial level. The university was fortunate to secure as first holder of this new chair a scholar of international eminence, Professor David Daube FBA, who only vacated the position on appointment to the regius professorship of civil law at Oxford, one of the most prestigious chairs in that university. Daube's presence in Aberdeen was an immense source of illumination in very many directions. His profound Jewish learning enabled him, for instance, to make, while he was amongst us, a permanently valuable contribution to the study of Christian origins in his seminal work—*The New Testament and Rabbinic Judaism*. In 1956 Daube was succeeded by his pupil and lecturer, Professor Peter Stein FBA, who in his turn left Aberdeen for a distinguished chair in his own University of Cambridge.

Certainly, as the fifties drew to their close, expansion was urgently needed to extend Aberdeen's energies as well as to secure its survival. It may be that some part of the present disasters would have been avoided, if the problem of reconciling regional role with contributions to the nationwide research obligations of the university community had been more clearly defined. But none could have foreseen the brutal, philistine style of the Thatcherite government—with classics, music (developed by

Barrett-Ayres on the foundations laid by Willan Swainson), Scandinavian studies, Italian, mediaeval studies, diminished or totally abandoned. It is sad for me to include history and philosophy of science in the casualty list, as I had some share in the initiation of this department, and the appointment of Dr W P D Wightman as the first lecturer. In the inter-disciplinary senior seminar he mounted, we had a veritable paradigm of the kind of development urgently needed nationwide in the 1960s—and in the 1990s. This growth point has now been snuffed out by UGC *diktat*.

A very real source of strength in the period 1947–60 was found in the remarkable succession of Gifford Lecturers: Professor John Wisdom; M Gabriel Marcel; Professor Michael Polanyi; Professor Paul Tillich; Professor H A Hodges; Professor H H Price. No university could be written off as simply provincial that attracted such men to its lecture theatres. And there was also the sadly short-lived Ritson Lectureship in international politics, which brought to Aberdeen such men as R H S Crossman, MP (1948), Alan Bullock (later Lord Bullock) (1950), and Lord Vansittart (1951).

We need to look realistically at the past, especially noting the 'might-have-beens'. In our failures lay in part Thatcher's opportunity to impose (through the UGC working within the framework government had laid down) her crudely materialist values on our life, even as the trade unions' arrogant and brutish cruelty in the 'winter of discontent' of 1978–9 gave her the chance to obliterate the post-war consensus in the interest of confrontation, and an ever deepening centralised authoritarianism. Yet we had our successes in Aberdeen University, and it is perhaps permissible for me to end by remarking that of the six who worked with me in the small but ancient department of moral philosophy between 1947 and 1960, before I left in the autumn of 1960, one had gone to an Oxford fellowship (succeeding Professor R C Cross at Jesus College Oxford, when Cross succeeded Ferguson in 1953 in the logic chair), and two to chairs (A G N Flew to Keele in 1954, and R W Hepburn to Nottingham in 1960). All are highly distinguished; and to Professor Hepburn, now in Edinburgh, who entered Aberdeen University as a student in the autumn of 1947, and was wholly trained here both as a student and as a junior academic, members of the university philosophical community in the UK owe much for the strong defence mounted on that subject's behalf to the UGC.

Chapter 2

Contributions to the Regional Economy: Expenditure and Employment Aspects

ALEXANDER G KEMP and SANDRA J GALBRAITH

I   Introduction

The University of Aberdeen has for long been proud of its firm integration into the local region of which it forms a conspicuous part. The links with the surrounding communities are not only academic but social, cultural and economic. A very high proportion of local school leavers embarking on university education have traditionally made Aberdeen University a leading choice. Many graduates have obtained employment locally. The current and capital expenditures of the university, its staff, and its students have constituted major injections into the local economy. The university has also directly employed local people in a variety of posts. Links with the regional economy also exist as a consequence of the provision of courses with specific local application. Similarly, some research and consultancy work has been undertaken to meet the needs of local industries. Courses have also been provided to satisfy local cultural and social interests.

In this paper the expenditure and employment aspects of the university's economic role in the local region since the Second World War are examined. Where possible attempts are made to quantify or measure the university's impact. The changing nature of its impact over the long period relating to expenditure and employment is highlighted. The university's impact is defined to include that of its students and graduates as well as its own employees.

II   Local Economic Role of the University: Conceptual Issues

(a) University Expenditure and the Local Economy

The expenditure of the University of Aberdeen constitutes a significant injection of spending power into the local region. The relevant expenditure is the total increase in spending which takes place in the region as a consequence of the existence of the university. The precise effects of this expenditure on the local economy depend not only on the total size of the outlays in question but on the type of expenditure. The second and subsequent round effects of the initial spending are also relevant elements in the total impact. In economic analysis the initial income source which is injected into the economy is conventionally termed the multiplicand, and the subsequent respending of that income is the multiplier effect. The total impact on the economy depends on the size of the values for both the multiplicand and multiplier.

In the case of Aberdeen University over the long period under review there are several components of the appropriate multiplicand which may usefully be considered separately. Initial direct injections into the local economy emanate from (1) university expenditure on (a) capital items, (b) materials, (c) the salary and wage bill of members of staff, and (2) the expenditure of university students.

These items are clearly relevant initial injections, but other items can possibly be included. If members of staff have retired and continue to live in the local region because of their previous link with the university, expenditure from their pensions could be regarded as an appropriate initial injection. The expansion of the university will have induced investment expenditure elsewhere in the local economy. This will have been in the construction of extra capacity in both the private and public sectors to meet the additional demands emanating from that expansion. A major university stimulates significant immigration into the local region. In turn this necessitates an increase in the local economy's productive capacity to provide goods and services such as housing, retail distribution, education and health services, and many other miscellaneous services.

In conventional economic analysis this induced investment expenditure is not normally regarded as a multiplicand. However, Brownrigg[1] and Greig[2] in two separate papers have argued that it is convenient to include induced investment as a type of multiplicand. It is acknowledged that the nature of this multiplicand is quite different from the conventional type.

It is important to distinguish between the various types of multiplicand as their effects on the local economy are not the same. So far as capital expenditure is concerned, outlays on construction work will generally cause a temporary increase in economic activity. Expenditure on equipment will be of a more regularly recurring nature. The amount of spending will generally be related to several factors including the capacity of the institution, the type of teaching and research activity, and the pace of technical progress and obsolescence of the equipment concerned. Expenditure on materials is not investment in the conventional sense, but from the perspective of its role as a multiplicand it is very similar. The amount will be a function of the capacity of the university, and the type of teaching and research being undertaken.

In conventional regional economic analysis the total expenditure on investment (and materials in this case) does not constitute the appropriate multiplicand. This is because part of the initial outlay will immediately leave the region in the purchase of imports. Thus equipment may be imported as may construction materials. The convention is to define the appropriate multiplicand as $I(1-M)$, where I is the value of the total investment expenditure and M is the proportion spent on imports from outside the region. The size of this initial leakage is a function of several factors including, in particular, the size of the region and its industrial structure.

The size of the initial leakage is also a function of the particular type of expenditure. Purchases of highly specialised scientific or medical equipment are very likely to be met from sources outwith the north east of Scotland: much of the expenditure is an immediate leak from the region. On the other hand investment in new construction projects is quite likely to result in a high proportion of the initial expenditure taking place within the region.

The university wage and salary bill constitutes a second injection into the local economy. Academic staff will almost certainly be comprised of people who are either immigrants into the region, or who would have migrated from the region had not the university been there to provide employment. Non-academic staff are unlikely to be immigrants into the region. They are much more likely to be local people. Further, compared to academic staff these employees are much less likely to leave the region if employment at the university were not available to them. It is more likely that they would seek employment elsewhere in the region. They might well have obtained jobs elsewhere in the region currently held by other people. Some employees, possibly among the cleaning and catering staff, could have been unemployed in the absence of the university. The distinction between (1) staff who either immigrate into the region or refrain from emigrating because the university exists, and (2) those who would in any case remain in the region, is particularly important when considering the likely size of the induced investment. For purposes of the present study it is the extra injection into the local economy resulting from the presence of the university which is relevant.

The wage and salary bill is obviously an injection but, following the convention adopted when considering capital expenditure, the employer's National Insurance and superannuation contributions can be deducted. On this basis the appropriate multiplicand becomes $WS(1-ED)$ where WS is the gross wage and salary bill of the university and ED is the proportion deducted for the employer's National Insurance and super-annuation contributions.

The expenditure of students is a relevant injection into the local economy. There are both local and non-local students. In the present context this distinction is significant. Non-local students may make more demands on the regon's infrastructure, particularly with regard to accom-modation. It is also very likely that the great majority of local students would have left the region to become students elsewhere in the absence of the university, so reducing their demands on the local infrastructure. Non-local students are much more likely to leave the region during vacations, and in that event their injections into the local economy will be less.

Students obtain their spending power from several sources including grants, parental contributions, borrowing and vacation earnings. So far as grants are concerned it is the maintenance component which is relevant here. (The fee component is income to the university and is reflected in its expenditure.) Parental contributions also constitute an injection. Where students are non-local this is obvious. On the assumption that local students would have gone outside the region in the absence of Aberdeen University their parental contributions would have gone with them, and so their continued presence in the region retains this spending power.

Some staff and students might live outside the local region. In such cases their total expenditures will not be initiated within the local economy. The importance of the university obviously depends upon the chosen definition of the local region: the direct effect of the university is obviously much greater in the Aberdeen economy than it is in the whole of the Grampian region. The multiplier effect of the university's spending will also be greater the bigger the size of the defined regional economy. Nevertheless the leakage from the Aberdeen economy is probably not much less than from the Grampian region as a whole: if the income is not respent within Aberdeen itself, it will probably flow outside the whole north-east region.

There are some possibilities of double counting. For example, students and staff incur expenditure on catering, hall and refectory charges within the university campus. Much of this spending will be on the wages and salaries of university employees. This is already included in the university wage and salary bill. Clearly only the net figure is relevant. As noted already, expenditure on fees is also reflected in university expenditure. With these modifications the injection of students' expenditure (S) is a relevant multiplicand.

The value of the injection representing induced investment depends upon a number of factors, principally (a) the size of the change in local income levels from the expenditure of staff and students, (b) the amount of excess capacity already existing in the relevant public and private service sectors, (c) the degree to which any expansion in staff and student numbers takes the form of immigration into the region, and (d) the size and industrial structure of the region.

It will normally be reasonable to assume that the infrastructure capacity is sufficient to meet only the needs of the indigenous population. Any increased investment in infrastructure capacity is then a function of the increase in the size of the incomes of immigrant staff and students. Any increase in student immigration and expenditure on accommodation, food, etcetera in halls of residence is reflected in university expenditure and does not, of course, constitute a further demand on the local community's infrastructure. The value of induced investment (ID) can be represented as rG where r is the community's capital:output ratio (which allows the feedback effects of induced investment to be calculated), and G represents the incomes of immigrant university staff and students. Immigrants will constitute a proportion of staff and students. Thus $G = g[WS(1-ED)+S]$. Following the convention used when discussing university capital expenditure, there will also be an initial leakage from induced investment into imports of equipment and materials from outside the region. The total multiplicand now becomes $I(1-M)+[WS(1-ED)+S][1+rg(1-M)]$.

There are significant differences in the nature of the impact of the various injections on the local economy. Thus the effects of construction expenditure on new building will be to cause a temporary increase in local economic activity. The same applies to the effects of induced investment in the infrastructure. Expenditure on materials, equipment and wages and salaries will (hopefully) be continuous and cause a permanent increase in local economic activity. The distinction is between the 'temporary' and 'final size' impact effects of expenditure.

The total increase in local economic activity depends on the size both of the initial injection and of the multiplier which measures the effects of the respending of the initial expenditure. The intial expenditure raises the level of local incomes. The recipients in turn increase their expenditure, causing a secondary increase in income. The process continues with the end result that the initial injection causes a multiple increase in incomes.

The size of the multiplier depends upon values of the leakages at each stage. There will be leakages into saving, taxation (direct and indirect), reduced social security benefits received, and imports from outside the region. More formally the required income multiplier is:

$$k_r = \frac{1}{1-c(1-t_d-b)(1-m-t_i)}$$

where c = marginal propensity to consume
$\quad t_d$ = marginal propensity to pay direct taxes
$\quad b$ = marginal rate of reduction in receipt of social security benefits
$\quad m$ = marginal propensity to import from outside the local region
$\quad t_i$ = marginal propensity to pay indirect taxes.

Marginal income tax rates over the long period have varied considerably in line with national policies. In any one year they also vary with the level of income of the recipient. Thus the structure of university employment influences the size of this leakage. Similarly, the rate at which social security benefits are reduced as people move into employment has varied considerably over the period. It will also depend upon the type of employment being generated: a part–time cleaner may continue to receive benefits on taking up employment at the university while a professor would be much less likely to receive benefits. The value of the propensity to import goods and services from outside the region depends on the size of the region and its industrial/commercial structure.

In the study by Brownrigg[3] on the impact of the University of Stirling on its local economy values for k_r of 1.24 and 1.54 have been employed. In a very recent study employing input:output analysis the Fraser of Allander Institute estimates a GDP multiplier for the effect of reduced expenditure by the University of Aberdeen of 1.75 for the whole of Scotland.[4]

The effect of university expenditure on local employment can also be calculated. This will be the sum of direct and indirect employment. Local employment multipliers can be estimated in the same way that local income multipliers are calculated. Following Brownrigg[5] indirect employment can be estimated as follows:

$$\Delta E_i = \frac{E_d W_d (1 - s - t)(1 - m) + k - 1}{L}$$

where
$\quad \Delta E_i$ = change in indirect employment
$\quad E_d$ = direct employment
$\quad W_d$ = wages of E_d
$\quad s$ = propensity to save
$\quad t$ = propensity to tax
$\quad m$ = propensity to import
$\quad k$ = income multiplier
$\quad L$ = income needed to create an additional job

More complex formulations can be constructed. In actual calculations it is convenient to estimate a 'direct employee equivalent' for students. Using the formula outlined above, Brownrigg estimated a regional employment multiplier of 1.36 for Stirling University at the construction stage,[6] and one of 1.7 when further indirect effects from public sector employment are included.

(b) *Local Employment of Aberdeen Graduates*

The University of Aberdeen has always contributed to the local economy by providing a source of skilled labour, but its quantitative significance has never been adequately measured and elucidated. An attempt to quantify the university's contribution in this respect involves estimating (a) the numbers of graduates sent into employment in the region, and (b) the type of employment generated. Some indication can then be obtained of the responsiveness of the university to the changing needs of the local economy.

The relative importance of the local economy as a source of employment for the university's graduates depends upon the definition of the region employed. In this study Grampian Region has been used as a convenient definition.

III   Empirical Investigation and Results

(a) *University Expenditure*

(1) *Data Sources*

Information on expenditure by the university was obtained from the University of Aberdeen Annual Accounts. These accounts are not prepared in such a way as to enable expenditures under the headings required for this study to be easily extracted. Further, accounting conventions have varied considerably over the period. To obtain relevant and consistent series much investigation and manipulation of the data at a disaggregated level was necessary. This was particularly the case with regard to wages and salaries. The total bill is now shown separately, and most categories of expenditure—for example, 'Heat, light, water and power' and 'Repairs and general maintenance'—contain elements of wages and salaries.

In recent years the format adopted in the university accounts has highlighted the General Revenue Account. On the expenditure side the main headings include Academic Departments, Academic Services, General Educational Expenditure, Premises, Administrative and Central Services, Staff and Student Facilities, Capital Expenditure from Revenue, Pensions, Transfers to other Account, Miscellaneous, Research Grants and Contracts and Other Services Rendered.

The accounts do not show the total university expenditure which is required for purposes of this study. Expenditure from the Equipment Account, Capital Expenditure Account (apart from that relating directly to revenue), and the Halls and Catering Account have been added and included. The university also obtains funds from various endowments. Where the expenditure has not been included under other accounts it has been included.

Transfers between accounts are a recurring feature of the university accounting system. For present purposes these have been netted out. Similarly transfers to reserves have been excluded. Sometimes an item of expenditure is shown net of an associated revenue. Again the full expenditure has been calculated.

Over the fifty year period much inflation has been experienced. With this in mind the various expenditure series were all revalued to 1988 prices using an appropriate price index.

(2) *Results*

On the basis of the exercise described above, various time series of university expenditure in real terms were calculated. In Chart 1 capital expenditure over the period is shown. This includes spending on equipment as well as construction. The most obvious feature is the dramatic rise and fall of expenditure in the period 1960–75. This was the period of rapid expansion in the capacity of the university with the greatest level of activity being in the period 1960–6. At its peak capital expenditure was approaching £15 million per year at 1988 prices.

Construction of new buildings constituted by far the most important element of capital expenditure in the whole period 1960–75. Construction work is fairly labour intensive. Further, it is understood that the great majority of contracts were awarded to locally based companies. It can safely be said that the effect in terms of local employment generation in this sector was very substantial.

The level of capital expenditure in recent years has been very much lower. There has been little new construction, but a considerable amount of refurbishment of existing buildings has occurred. A higher proportion of the expenditure has also gone on equipment. It is likely that much of this is imported into the region and so the benefits to the local economy have been somewhat less.

In Chart 2 the total wage and salary bill of the university at 1988 prices is shown for the period. The fast acceleration in both the academic and non-academic bills in the period 1962–75 is noteworthy. This reflects the increase in the numbers of staff and not a major rise in rates of pay! The dip in the second half of the 1970s reflects pay restraint, while the fall in the early 1980s is a consequence both of staff cuts and pay restraint. At its peak the annual total bill exceeds £32 million at 1988 prices.

The numbers of university employees have expanded enormously since the Second World War. Unfortunately no complete, consistent series is available, with data on numbers of non-academic staff only being available for relatively recent years. Just after the Second World War there were 150 academic (or 179 academic plus academic-related) staff. Academic staff numbered 297 in 1960–1, 704 in 1970–1, 887 in 1980–1 and 776 in 1987–8. Total university employees numbered 2,755 at the end of 1984, and 2,480 at the end of 1988.

In Chart 3 the total expenditure of the university over the period is shown. This includes not only the wage and salary bill and capital expenditure, but also expenditure on a large number of miscellaneous items such as purchase of materials, paper, fuel, books, and halls and catering. It also includes expenditure on local rates. This last—and large—item is best regarded as an injection into the local economy although it is a tax. Expenditure on rates by the university in effect comes from outside the region via the UGC grant. From the viewpoint of the local authority it represents income which permits either local services to be (marginally) increased or rate poundages elsewhere to be (marginally) reduced. In either case the net effect is an injection into the local economy. At its peak annual total expenditure has approached £56 million in 1988 prices.

Unsurprisingly total expenditure grew most rapidly in the period 1961–6. The dips in the second half of the 1970s and the first few years of the 1980s reflect the fall in the wage and salary bill. Obviously in the last decade the expenditure has become more dominated by the wage and salary bill than it was in the 1960s.

A considerable amount of further information is required before accurate estimates of the total local income generated by university expenditure can be made. In particular data on the various import leakages are needed. These will also have altered over the period because of the changing structure of the expenditure. The total university expenditure of around £56 million in 1987–8 can be compared with gross expenditure of £94.6 million by Aberdeen District Council in the same year.

Regarding total local employment generated by the university expenditure, employment multipliers of the order of 1.36 and 1.7 which were employed in the Stirling study could be relevant for Aberdeen. If anything, the local multiplier effect in Aberdeen might be slightly higher.

(b) *Students' Expenditure*

It has not been possible directly to estimate the expenditure of students. An indication has been obtained from information regarding student grants and the numbers of students attending the university. Statistics on full-time student numbers were taken from various publications of the University Grants Committee. Statistics on student maintenance grants (maximum) were obtained from the Scottish Education Department. Data were available from 1962.

The value of the grant over the period was converted to 1988 prices using the retail price index. The real value of the grant has shown a trend to decrease over the period (at 1988 prices from £2,500 in 1962 to £1,900 in 1987–8). Total student numbers grew substantially in the 1960s, and thereafter exhibited very modest growth.

The resulting total real expenditure (on the assumption that all the grant income was spent) is shown in Chart 4. Any significant growth has reflected increases in student numbers. Peak expenditure occurred in the late 1970s when it attained annual levels in excess of £12.5 million. The significant decline in the early 1980s coincided with a period of only modest decreases in student numbers.

The total expenditure of university and students combined in 1987–8 was around £67.6 million. There is some double-counting here as a considerable part of students' expenditure is on halls and catering services. A large share of these costs is composed of wages and salaries paid by the university. If this element of the wage and salary bill is excluded the total expenditure is around £63.5 million in 1987–8.

(c) Employment of University of Aberdeen Graduates

(1) Data: 1937–8 — 1970

Information on the employment of graduates 1938–70 was obtained from two volumes of the Roll of Graduates.[7] The sampling procedure was to select all the entries on every second page of the first Roll and from 75 per cent of the pages of the second Roll. (More entries were included for the second Roll because it was found that the total number of entries in the early years of the second Roll was rather small.) Entries which did not contain relevant information about employment (either type or location) were ignored. The resulting average sample sizes were 42.5 per cent for the first Roll and 47.25 per cent for the second one.

The objective was to estimate the employment of Aberdeen graduates in the local region. The local region was defined as that currently constituting Grampian Region. Graduates who had significant local employment were defined as those who had such employment for a minimum of two years.

The data produced as a result of the exercise described tended to show significant yearly fluctuations. Since the objective was to detect significant trends, a three-year moving average was calculated. This has been used in all the charts shown below.

(2) *Results: 1945–70*

In Chart 5 estimates of the absolute numbers of graduates obtaining significant employment in the North East in the period 1952–69 are shown. (Full data are not available for the earlier years.) The obvious striking feature is the large increase in the numbers obtaining local employment in the 1960s. This growth was spread across a number of types of employment. There was noteworthy growth in local employment in teaching, medicine, academic/research work, industry and commerce.

A further indication of the relative importance of local employment is seen from Chart 6 which shows the proportion of graduates with significant employment in the North East. In the early post-war years in excess of 40 per cent worked in the North East. Chart 6 shows a downward trend in the relative importance of the local labour market in the 1960s though the absolute numbers were generally increasing. The university was a significant exporter of graduates throughout the period, but this became more pronounced in the years of expansion in the 1960s.

Throughout the period the teaching profession constituted by far the most important local type of employment for graduates. In Chart 7 the proportion of local graduate employment represented by teaching over the period is shown. The share is seen frequently to exceed 50 per cent and sometimes 60 per cent. Although the share falls in the 1960s it is still over 40 per cent by 1970. The absolute numbers also increased sharply in the 1960s.

Over the period the absolute numbers employed locally in medicine showed a moderate increase. The relative importance of medicine as a source of local employment for graduates is shown in Chart 8. Its share fluctuated considerably from a high of 24 per cent to 12 per cent. The marked volatility of employment in other sectors of the local economy is partly responsible for the result.

Academic/research work has for long been well established in north-east Scotland. It is no surprise to find that this constitutes the next most important category of local graduate employment. In Chart 9 the relative importance of this type of work is shown over the period. This share exhibits some fluctuation and a broad upward trend. On average this source of employment has accounted for 10 per cent to 12 per cent of jobs for locally employed graduates.

The share of local graduate employment in industry and commerce (excluding oil and oil-related activities) is shown in Chart 10. There is seen to be a significant growth in the first half of the 1950s followed by a fall until the mid 1960s. The absolute numbers employed locally in industry/commerce also fell in this period. This may have been due to the very limited new industrial development in the period in the Aberdeen area, coupled with the fact that traditional industries tended not to employ many graduates. In the later 1960s there was a significant absolute and relative increase in the importance of industry as a local source of graduate employment.

The relative contribution of law, accountancy and the church to local graduate employment is shown in Chart 11. (The individual share of each is very small.) The absolute number employed in these three professions shows an absolute increase in the 1960s (with law being the most important growth area).

The relative importance of all other types of graduate employment was relatively low over the period. At the end of the period construction, primary industry and oil/oil-related work were beginning to become a significant source of local employment for graduates. Interestingly agriculture was a more important source of local graduate employment at the end of the period than it was in earlier years.

(3) Data: 1972–87

For the period since 1972 data on the 'first destination' of graduates is available from the records of the University Careers and Appointments Office. A 50 per cent sample from the records of the Careers Office was taken. Where inadequate or zero information regarding the destination or type of employment of the graduate was given the entry was ignored. The total number of graduates included in the sample was 7,560, of which 3,388 had their first destination in the North East.

A large number of new graduates have their first destination in further training. This was defined as a non-salary-earning activity. Thus trainee accountants and medical house officers were defined to be in employment. The 'further training' category was subdivided into 'teacher training', 'Diploma in Legal Practice' (DLP), and 'other PG'.

For the year 1979–80 the records of the Careers Office were destroyed. The average figures for 1978–9 and 1980–1 were employed for guidance. Records are also incomplete for law graduates for 1975–6 and 1976–7.

(4) Results: 1972–87

Estimates have been made of the absolute numbers of graduates making the North East their first destination. The annual number reached a peak of nearly 800 in 1985, while the lowest figure was just below 600. In Chart 12 the numbers proceeding into further training are shown, split between 'teacher training', 'DLP', and 'other PG'. The numbers proceeding into teacher training are seen to fall dramatically over the period, reflecting the falling employment opportunities.

Since the DLP commenced the absolute numbers proceeding to this form of further training have remained comparatively steady. The numbers proceeding to other postgraduate work in the region have fluctuated rather more.

In Chart 13 the estimated numbers of graduates proceeding (a) to further training and (b) to employment in the North East are shown. At the start of the period the numbers proceeding to further training locally greatly exceeded those obtaining direct employment. By the end of the period this situation was reversed. There has been an upward trend in the absolute numbers obtaining direct employment locally.

The *relative* importance of the North East as a destination for graduates has been decreasing, however. In Chart 14 the proportion of total graduates being locally based is shown. The decrease is quite marked. The university has increasingly become an exporter of graduates over the period.

The relative importance of further training for locally based graduates is shown in Chart 15. There was a sharp decline in the early part of the period followed by some increase in the late 1970s and early 1980s. The decline in the relative importance of teaching is further highlighted in Chart 16, which shows the proportion of locally based graduates who made this activity their first destination.

The fall in teacher training as a local destination has been partially offset by the rise in the relative importance of the DLP. The proportion of locally based graduates who made this their first destination is shown in Chart 17. The relative importance of other types of postgraduate training is shown in Chart 18. Its share at the end of the period was as high as it was at the beginning.

The relative importance of direct employment as a first destination for locally based graduates has increased significantly over the period. This is seen from Chart 19. At the beginning of the period around 40 per cent of locally based new graduates were entering direct employment. By the end of the period it was in the range 50 per cent to 60 per cent.

Industry and commerce (including primary industry, but excluding law and accountancy) have become increasingly important over the period. In Chart 20 there is an upward trend in the proportion of locally based graduates becoming employed in industry and commerce.

Within this category the oil and oil-related sectors have become more important. In Chart 21 the proportion of locally based graduates proceeding to employment in this sector is shown. There was a very marked increase in the absolute numbers entering this sector in the early 1980s. The fall in the last couple of years reflects the recession in the industry in 1986 and 1987 caused by the collapse in oil prices.

Over the last two decades national employment in the services sector has expanded significantly. Local employment of graduates in the private commercial, financial, and miscellaneous services sector (excluding law and accountancy) has also grown significantly since the early 1970s. On average it has more than doubled in the 1980s compared to the 1970s. But when the details of the employment of people in this group were examined, it was found that a significant number were working in activities not normally associated with graduates. Taxi drivers and shop assistants are examples. This reflects the problem of graduate unemployment which developed in this period. In Chart 22 the proportion of locally based graduates whose first destination was this miscellaneous group is shown.

Reflecting the growth in financial services, the employment of locally based graduates in the accountancy profession has increased dramatically, particularly in the 1980s. The share of locally based graduates making the accountancy profession their first destination is shown in Chart 23. The dramatic increase in recent years is clearly seen.

The absolute numbers of locally based graduates entering employment (not training) in academic/research institutions has on average been higher in the 1980s than it was in the 1970s. The proportion of such graduates making such work their first destination is shown in Chart 24. The cutbacks in government funded expenditure in academic/research institutions in the North East have not had a noticeable effect on the absolute numbers of new graduates employed in this field of activity.

The absolute numbers of locally based graduates employed in medicine have increased since the early 1970s, but since then there has been no obvious trend. The proportion of such graduates making employment in medicine their first destination has averaged around 15 per cent, as shown in Chart 25.

Employment locally in public services has been the first destination of a moderate but significant absolute number of graduates in the period. On average it has constituted around 4 per cent. Employment in the law profession constitutes a significant outlet for local graduates. The introduction of the DLP has meant that the proportion directly entering employment in the law profession has fallen dramatically. In the 1980s it has been averaging 1 per cent of the first destinations of local graduates.

IV   Conclusion

It is clear from this study that the expenditure of the university and its students has constituted an increasingly important injection into the local economy. The dramatic increase in its importance took place in the second half of the 1960s in the era of major capacity expansion. The sharp drop in capital expenditure in the 1980s was broadly compensated by growth in other forms of expenditure, with the result that total university spending reached an historic peak in real terms of around £56 million in 1987–8.

The structure of the expenditure has changed markedly. In the late 1960s construction expenditure was a major component, but in recent years the spending pattern has been dominated by the wage and salary bill, materials and equipment. The local construction industry was a major beneficiary of university expenditure in the 1960s, but now suppliers of consumer goods and services, materials and equipment obtain the greatest benefits.

While the real value of the student grant has fallen continuously since the early 1960s, total student expenditure grew in real terms through much of the 1960s due to the sharp increase in numbers. It has fallen from its peak in the late 1970s, and expenditure of maintenance grants (on the assumption that the full grant was received) was £11.6 million in 1987–8. It is appreciated that students' expenditure is also financed by other means such as bank loans, but no estimates of these are available.

When the double counting of students' expenditure on halls and catering and the spending by the university on these services is taken into account, the total expenditure of the university plus students (as defined) was around £63.5 million in 1987–8. As an indication of its relative importance the gross expenditure of Aberdeen District Council in 1987–8 was £94.6 million.

The university is clearly seen to be an important producer of skilled labour in demand in the North East as evidenced by the numbers of graduates employed locally. The results provide some evidence to support the view that it has responded to the changing pattern of demand for skills. The rapid growth in employment in accountancy has been accompanied by a major expansion in graduate output in that discipline. Similarly, the university has been able to contribute significantly to the increased demand for graduates emanating from the offshore oil industry.

The results of the analysis of graduate employment also show that the university increasingly became an exporter of graduates following the major expansion in student numbers. This is probably due not only to the supply of graduates exceeding local demand to a greater extent than previously, but also to a higher proportion of graduates originating from outside the North East. They probably have a lower propensity to stay in the local region.

Though difficult to quantify, the presence of graduates from the university can claim to have improved the efficiency of the local labour market, and made some contribution to the performance of locally based industries. These claims are best substantiated by a consideration of the local labour market in the 1970s. In this decade the upsurge in oil-related activity was very sharp. It created very considerable labour shortages for both incoming and locally established firms. There was considerable strain on the infrastructure particularly with regard to housing. For a time a vicious circle existed whereby firms had difficulty in importing skilled labour because of the housing shortage, while the construction industry had difficulty in expanding because of the shortage of construction workers and could not import workers because of the housing shortage!

Against this background, the availability of local graduates must have made a contribution to the alleviation of the problem. Locally based graduates were probably less likely to have a personal housing problem than potential employees from outside the region. Not only the expanding offshore supply and accountancy sectors noted above benefited from this factor, but all other employers requiring graduate labour.

In conclusion, the contribution of the University of Aberdeen to the economy of Aberdeen and the North East of Scotland since the Second World War has clearly been noteworthy. University and student expenditures have certainly had a major impact on the region over the years, and many graduates of the University of Aberdeen have been, and are economically active in the area. As one of the major institutions, and therefore employers, of the North East of Scotland, the University of Aberdeen can claim to have played a central role in the economic life of many residents in this area.

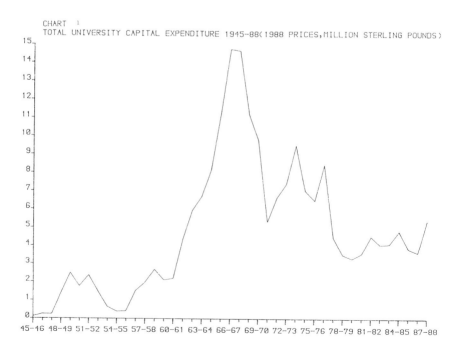

CHART   1
TOTAL UNIVERSITY CAPITAL EXPENDITURE 1945-88(1988 PRICES,MILLION STERLING POUNDS)

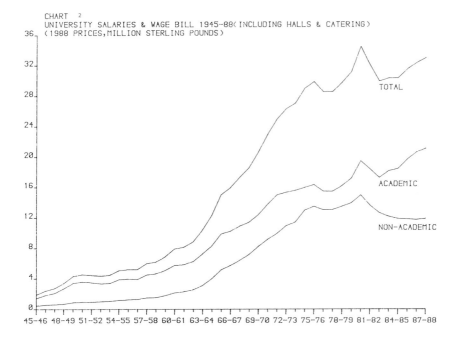

CHART   2
UNIVERSITY SALARIES & WAGE BILL 1945-88(INCLUDING HALLS & CATERING)
(1988 PRICES,MILLION STERLING POUNDS)

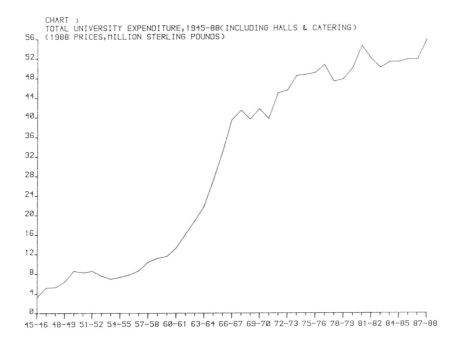

CHART 3
TOTAL UNIVERSITY EXPENDITURE,1945-88(INCLUDING HALLS & CATERING)
(1988 PRICES,MILLION STERLING POUNDS)

CHART 4
TOTAL (FULL-TIME) STUDENT EXPENDITURE 1962-88
(REAL 1988 PRICES,MILLION STERLING POUNDS)

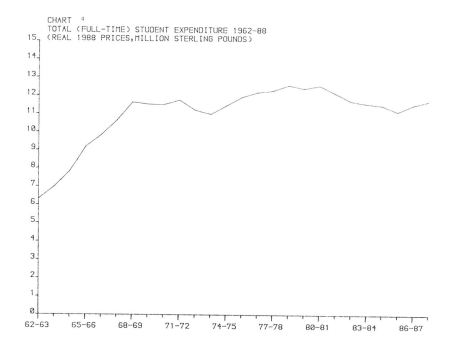

CHART 5
ESTIMATED NUMBERS OF GRADUATES WITH SIGNIFICANT EMPLOYMENT IN
NORTH-EAST SCOTLAND,(1952-1969)

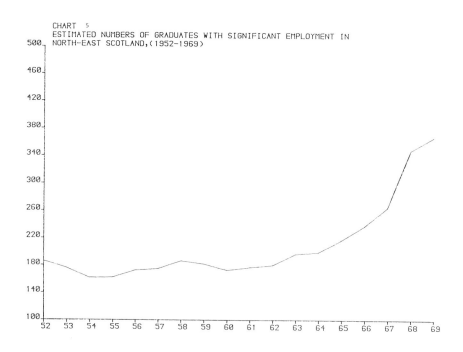

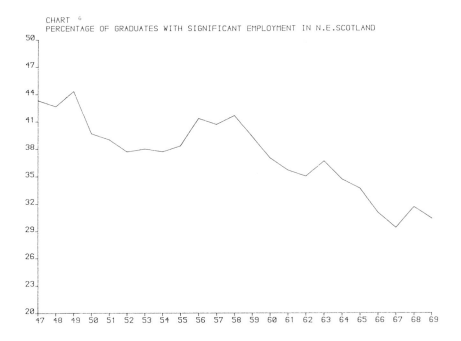

CHART 6
PERCENTAGE OF GRADUATES WITH SIGNIFICANT EMPLOYMENT IN N.E.SCOTLAND

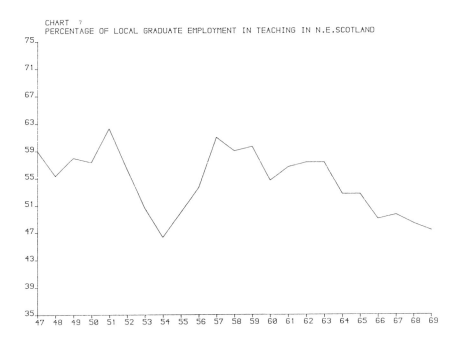

CHART 7
PERCENTAGE OF LOCAL GRADUATE EMPLOYMENT IN TEACHING IN N.E.SCOTLAND

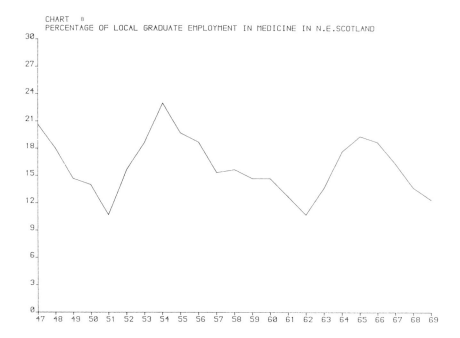

CHART   8
PERCENTAGE OF LOCAL GRADUATE EMPLOYMENT IN MEDICINE IN N.E.SCOTLAND

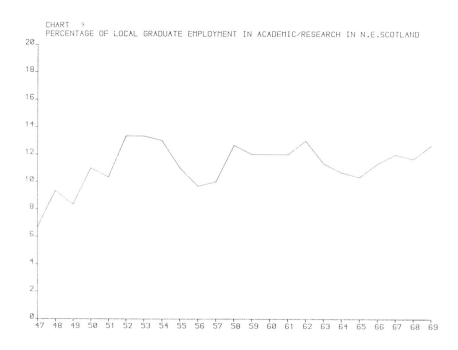

CHART   9
PERCENTAGE OF LOCAL GRADUATE EMPLOYMENT IN ACADEMIC/RESEARCH IN N.E.SCOTLAND

CHART 10
PERCENTAGE OF LOCAL GRADUATE EMPLOYMENT IN INDUSTRY/COMMERCE IN N.E.SCOTLAND

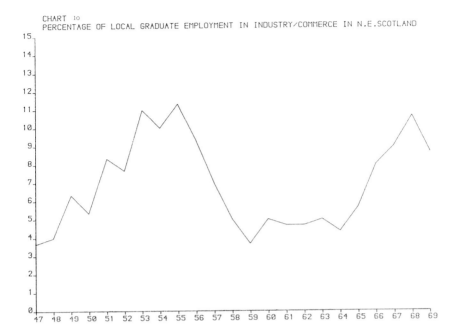

CHART 11
PERCENTAGE OF LOCAL GRADUATE EMPLOYMENT IN OTHER PROFESSIONS IN N.E.SCOTLAND
(LAW,ACCOUNTANCY,CHURCH)

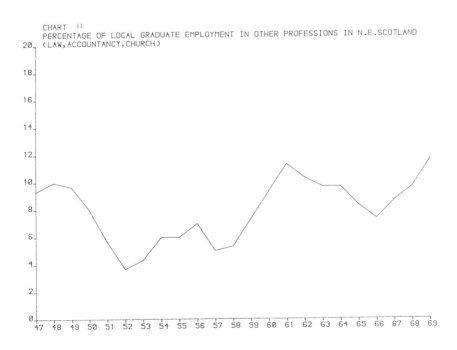

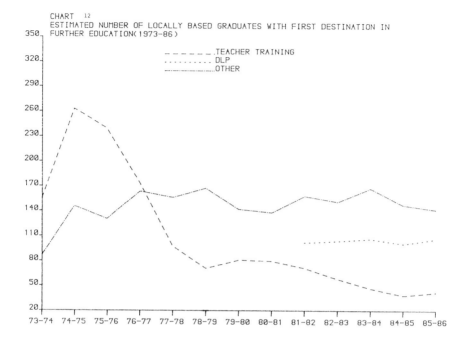

CHART 12
ESTIMATED NUMBER OF LOCALLY BASED GRADUATES WITH FIRST DESTINATION IN
FURTHER EDUCATION(1973–86)

_ _ _ _ _ _.TEACHER TRAINING
. . . . .DLP
._._._._._._.OTHER

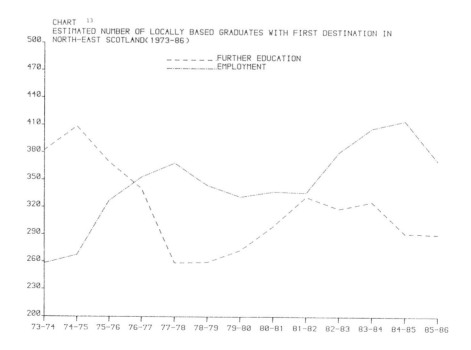

CHART 13
ESTIMATED NUMBER OF LOCALLY BASED GRADUATES WITH FIRST DESTINATION IN
NORTH-EAST SCOTLAND(1973–86)

_ _ _ _ _.FURTHER EDUCATION
._._._._._._.EMPLOYMENT

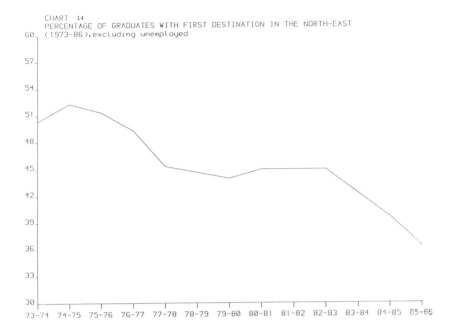

CHART 14
PERCENTAGE OF GRADUATES WITH FIRST DESTINATION IN THE NORTH-EAST
(1973-86),excluding unemployed

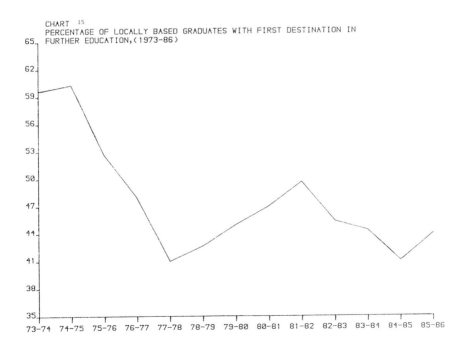

CHART 15
PERCENTAGE OF LOCALLY BASED GRADUATES WITH FIRST DESTINATION IN
FURTHER EDUCATION,(1973-86)

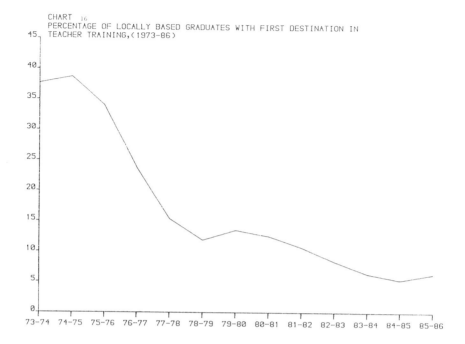

CHART 16
PERCENTAGE OF LOCALLY BASED GRADUATES WITH FIRST DESTINATION IN
TEACHER TRAINING,(1973-86)

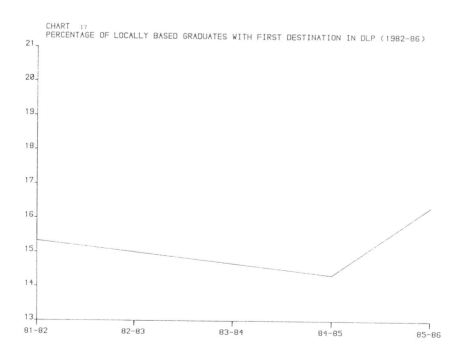

CHART 17
PERCENTAGE OF LOCALLY BASED GRADUATES WITH FIRST DESTINATION IN DLP (1982-86)

CHART 18
PERCENTAGE OF LOCALLY BASED GRADUATES WITH FIRST DESTINATION IN
OTHER POST-GRADUATE TRAINING,(1973-86)

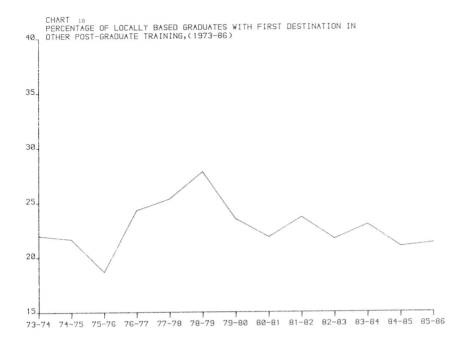

CHART   19
PERCENTAGE OF LOCALLY BASED GRADUATES WITH FIRST DESTINATION IN EMPLOYMENT(1973-86

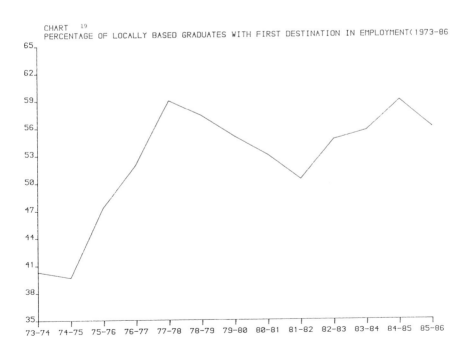

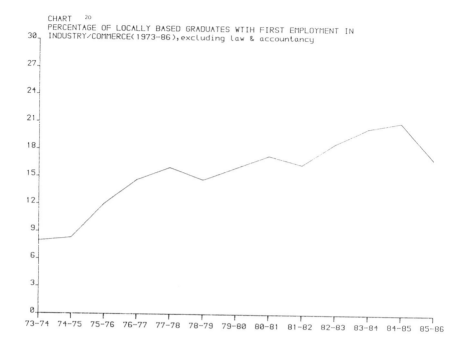

CHART   20
PERCENTAGE OF LOCALLY BASED GRADUATES WTIH FIRST EMPLOYMENT IN
INDUSTRY/COMMERCE(1973-86),excluding law & accountancy

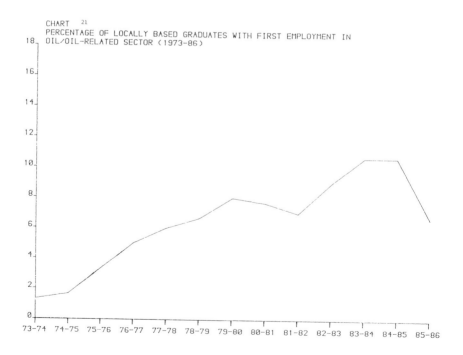

CHART   21
PERCENTAGE OF LOCALLY BASED GRADUATES WITH FIRST EMPLOYMENT IN
OIL/OIL-RELATED SECTOR (1973-86)

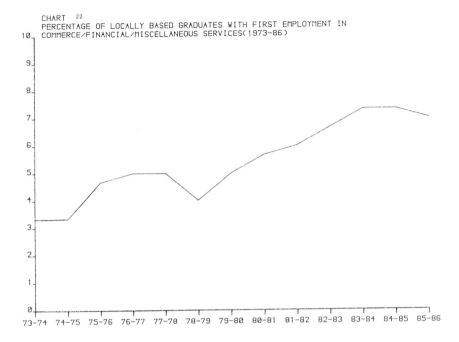

CHART 22
PERCENTAGE OF LOCALLY BASED GRADUATES WITH FIRST EMPLOYMENT IN
COMMERCE/FINANCIAL/MISCELLANEOUS SERVICES(1973-86)

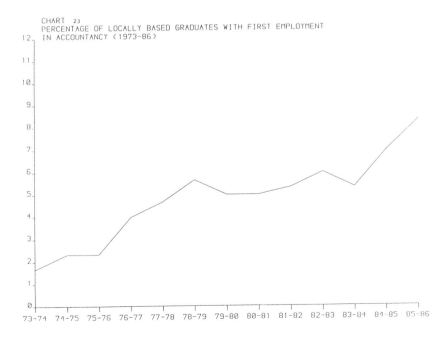

CHART 23
PERCENTAGE OF LOCALLY BASED GRADUATES WITH FIRST EMPLOYMENT
IN ACCOUNTANCY (1973-86)

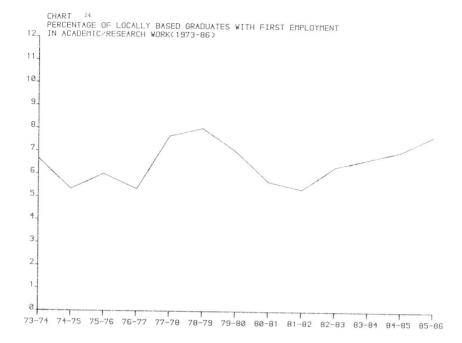

CHART 24
PERCENTAGE OF LOCALLY BASED GRADUATES WITH FIRST EMPLOYMENT
IN ACADEMIC/RESEARCH WORK(1973-86)

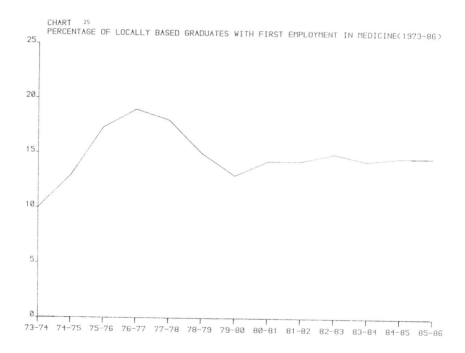

CHART 25
PERCENTAGE OF LOCALLY BASED GRADUATES WITH FIRST EMPLOYMENT IN MEDICINE(1973-86)

Chapter 3

The Medical School and Health Care in the Region

ROY WEIR

As well as participating in the general activities of the university community a medical school carries three specific responsibilities: namely to teach, research, and participate in the care of patients. These three responsibilities are deemed both essential and mutually supportive. The years between 1945 and 1981 cover a period of remarkable and rapid change, particularly in the facilities and techniques of patient care. Therefore the nature of the local circumstances within which all three responsibilities developed needs to be appreciated. This in turn provides the background against which the policies and achievements of the Aberdeen Medical School can be reviewed.

There can be no doubt that the adverse grading by the UGC of the Aberdeen Medical School over its research record during the final years of the period ending in 1981 had in turn a major impact on the health services of the area. The effects were twofold. First, and of immediate consequence, was a reduction in resources. Second, and more difficult to accommodate, were the sense of injustice, the misunderstandings and the frustration that arose.

Any description of the contribution of the university, and in particular of the Medical School, to health and health care in the region cannot ignore that setback, and immediately it raises the issue of deciding upon appropriate criteria against which, or the setting within which, to view these contributions.

Given that judgements have been made about the perceived research performance of various components of all universities, it may seem particularly perverse to fail to identify appropriate criteria. The explanation is that the criteria used were devised in retrospect; devised, in fact, long after and with scant regard for the events that determined the activities that were being valued. Indeed the ultimate decision to use implicit audit, in effect a very restricted list of crude statistics that could be estimated for each school irrespective of size or the extent and nature of other commitments, was in itself an indication of the difficulty of identifying an appropriate common rule for a series of institutions differing widely in the nature of their locations and associations.

The reality, of course, is that we are products of our history and our social interactions—which are, in fact, the next two points I wish to make. Although we have all been asked to review the period 1945-81 a number of events during the previous 20 years were of particular importance. It was a significant and fascinating period in its own right, but I intend only to identify and carry forward three points. The first relates to the quite unique site at Foresterhill, at that time on the outskirts of Aberdeen. It became a reality about 1922 with the earmarking within the total site of nearly 50 acres for a Joint Hospital Scheme and for the university. The second point was the extent, in those days, of local autonomy, decision making and, of course, fund raising. The involvement of the Scottish Office in Edinburgh was small, and, bar providing time for legislation, that of London almost nil—the primary initiative and powerful influence was the local network and the resulting close relationships between gown, town, county, and the wide variety of voluntary hospital authorities. The third event, which followed an earlier decision to resite the Children's Hospital, was the final fund raising campaign about 1928 that led to the actual building of the new Royal Infirmary at Foresterhill; because of that, in its turn, the university built the new Medical School on the same site which already housed the new Children's Hospital and thereby a nearly unique opportunity was set. An essential component of that opportunity that also needs to be recorded, was the extent of the collaboration that existed between the University Court and Infirmary Governors. Both groups, of course, had to find money for the new developments that were proposed, but in those days, through cross-membership and common purpose, very effective use was made of any resources that could be raised.

In addition to a joint site and joint appointments (which were actually introduced in 1920) there were also during the twenties and thirties a number of specific jointly funded ventures, including a cardiovascular department, a pathology laboratory, and a biochemical and clinical laboratory service. In those days job descriptions were refreshingly short and to the point, effectively enabling the joint employers to envisage almost two jobs for the price of one. So the scene is set, with a new general hospital, a new children's hospital, a new medical school and joint services all on the same site; indeed the structure that had been evolved in Aberdeen set the pattern for the rest of Scotland and was encouraged by incorporation in the Local Government Act of 1929. The fact that these facilities were not only in existence but were the established practice had a profound effect on what happened after the Second World War.

My second general point relates to social interaction; there is a view that medical services are determined by whims and fancies (if not self-centredness) on the part of the medical profession. Health care, however, merely reflects problems, values and expectations within society; what is happening in society by and large sets the limits within which the practice of a profession is determined. Some social commentators may consider that to be sophistry, or at the least special pleading, but the expectations of society itself are usually more practical and realistic.

Medicine has been no different. The major changes within society, to some extent before, but more markedly after the Second World War, which are significant to our consideration, include the changed age structure of the population, the narrowing of social differences, improved standards of living and expectations and the remarkable technical achievements of our age. The corresponding effects on health care have been that with an older population, with different disease distributions, and with new industrial and commercial opportunities, there is now intense competition for staff, especially young entrants. The technical advances of the pharmaceutical and equipment manufacturers have concentrated developments in hospitals. Confidence in ever-expanding technology has lessened the general commitment to prevention, and to exploit fully the new technology has required that more and more of the health professionals work in teams. As the prospects of new cures have appeared to grow, so the emphasis on risk-avoiding behaviour has declined. The final burden from the benefits of technology has been the speed of change and resulting obsolescence of even relatively new equipment and procedures.

Just taking the issue of speed: first there was the explosion in modern therapeutic agents with antibiotics changing the patterns of disease; with the pill releasing the 'fifth freedom'; and with cytotoxic agents and psychotropic drugs providing meaningful ways of arresting cancer and controlling personality disorders. Immediately following came the advent of transplantation and 'spare part' surgery, allowing replacement of limbs, kidneys, hearts, lungs, livers, joints and various physiological regulators. These advances in turn are also changing the dependency of patients who are no longer necessarily confined to hospital beds and who now seek and expect care in the community. This incidentally is a challenge to which the specialist services have not fully responded. Society is now faced with our implied ability to manipulate biochemical and genetic systems. All these have occurred in the period that we are considering.

I have already mentioned that health care reflects the problems and values of society and indeed this can be seen in the major concerns and developments of successive phases as our services have evolved over the last century and a half. One hundred and fifty years ago concern related to the welfare of the poor; it then changed about a hundred years ago to environmental and infectious disease control; and seventy years ago to basic medical care. The period covered by this review has seen a change to comprehensive medical care; then, as more and more became possible, to the organisation needed to deliver the benefits of care that technology offered; and now, almost inevitably, we are entering yet a further phase as we struggle with the problem of how modern health care should be financed.

I have spent a little time setting the scene and defining the background because as I have implied the current emphasis on research selectivity is mostly a matter of political expediency; the range of activities, within which the full contribution of the university to health care in the Region should be determined, is much wider than the pragmatic exercise of creating an apparent justification for moving resources. Certainly in this wider context two of the major areas of relevant activity relate first to the provision, locally, of comprehensive medical care, and second to the organisation of its effective delivery: key items in any real or meaningful assessment.

In a review of the period 1945–81 the emphasis inevitably, and also properly, must focus on the social legislation following almost immediately after the 1939–45 war. Within that series, the National Health Service Act of 1948 had quite profound effects on the university. At the end of the war, as explained above, there was a large fully serviced site, two new hospitals, a new medical school, a tradition over 20 years of close collaboration and a major change of staff as ex-service doctors returned to civilian practice. A particular opportunity was the salary given for a time to doctors discharged from the forces to attach themselves to a hospital, practice, or university to help restart their careers. This was then followed by the creation under the National Health Service of full-time consultant posts which allowed those doctors not wishing to do private practice to achieve reasonable incomes. These circumstances fostered in Aberdeen, as in other parts of Scotland, a widespread commitment to academic and specialist careers without recourse to private practice.

Perhaps the most significant local development in the delivery of health care had been launched during the 1930s. It had become apparent that to achieve comprehensive high quality obstetrical services, even in the face of a considerable rural population, a centrally controlled and co-ordinated policy would be necessary. There then followed the establishment of a remarkable obstetric service based on specialist care and centralised facilities. Ultimately linked to these services was a research programme which in its own right and in association with the Rowett Research Institute received international acclaim. Mothers and daughters of the third and fourth generations of the original families are still collaborating with the local obstetricians. The first Chairman of the new North-Eastern Regional Hospital Board, Dr May Baird, had had before appointment considerable experience as convener of the Local Authority Health Committee. Partly from this experience, partly because of the success of the obstetrical services, and partly because of geographical considerations, there evolved a policy which concentrated the majority of acute services in Aberdeen and particularly on the Foresterhill site.

A consequence of this policy was that although only 50 per cent of the population lived in or near Aberdeen, 80 per cent of the specialist services operated there. This concentration was far higher than in any other part of Scotland and the resulting economies of scale permitted expansion in the provision of acute services with fewer medical staff. In consequence a far wider range of services was possible within the overall budget and the concentration on or near one site was of tremendous benefit to under-graduate teaching and ensured the involvement of the university medical teachers in almost all aspects of the services.

Continuing close collaboration between Court and Board was a promi-nent feature of the early years and most service developments were jointly and often equally funded with the university. In consequence the Medical School employed virtually the total staff of the laboratory services for the area and in addition a number of the wards were entirely staffed by university doctors. Although a similar pattern was established in other parts of Scotland, the outcome varied, depending on the opportunity to concentrate facilities and on the location of the medical schools. Indeed at the end of the period under consideration, in absolute numbers over 17 per cent of the hospital consultants in Aberdeen were wholly in the employment of the university, similar to Edinburgh but well above Glas-gow at 10 per cent and Dundee at 9 per cent.

National comparative manpower statistics are notoriously difficult to interpret, not only because of changes in definitions and categories, but also because of unintentional (and sometimes intentional) variations in recording practices. Nonetheless it is still possible to identify major trends and anomalies. To demonstrate the implications of the developments referred to, three sets of figures have been abstracted. First, in Table 1 the growth in the clinical departments of the Aberdeen Medical School, currently termed Cost Centre 1, is shown from 1950 to 1980 and in-cludes all the academic and academic-related staff both medical and non-medical.

Second, Table 2 records for the same period the growth of consultant staff in Aberdeen and in Scotland as a whole, employed either wholly by the universities or by the Health Service. Finally in Table 3, a comparison is made at the end of the period being reviewed of the medical staff

TABLE 1   UNIVERSITY OF ABERDEEN MEDICAL SCHOOL STAFFING, 1950-90

Academic and Academic Related	1950	1960	1970	1980	1990[2]
Wholly employed[1]	27	48	100	121	(64)
Partly employed	21	54	12	7	(7)

1. Excluding Biomedical Physics and Engineering.
2. Planning Targets.

SOURCE: University Calendars 1950–80

employed by the Health Service or the university, expressed as rates per unit of health budget in the four teaching hospital areas of Scotland.

Table 1 shows the considerable growth and change in category of medically and non-medically qualified staff over the period. The part-time staff during the first half of the period were almost entirely Health Service senior consultant staff receiving relatively modest remuneration in respect of the organisation and supervision of bed-side and outpatient teaching. By the mid sixties few of the Health Service staff received any payment and these responsibilities had become part of a knock-for-knock arrangement by which facilities for teaching and research on the one hand, and service provision on the other, were deemed to equate. At the same time the Table shows a substantial increase in university staff able to provide and indirectly support the clinical services. As the services grew and the developments became more and more complex it also became increasingly difficult to rationalise, let alone test, the knock-for-knock assumptions. In 1980 over 100 of the 121 university staff were theoretically providing clinical services and, equally theoretically, 314 Health Service staff were teaching and receiving access to university facilities for schol-arship and research. A similar policy was, of course, being pursued right across the country. However the head-start that the Foresterhill complex and the pre-existing collaboration afforded Aberdeen at the beginning of the Health Service era meant that locally the process had gone faster and further. Given the unquantifiable scale these arrangements had reached, it was almost inevitable that the Treasury would finally decide that some form of meaningful cross-accounting had to be considered.

There were, however, other local features worth noting; Table 2 shows the rapid build up of senior staff employed wholly by the University of Aberdeen between 1960 and 1970 and that the new planning figures for 1990 bring the proportion of Health Service to university staff closer to the national average.

During the period clinical student numbers increased by 40 per cent from 425 to 600, while staff numbers increased by 300 per cent. That is not, of course, a totally valid comparison because in addition to the

TABLE 2 ALL MEDICALLY QUALIFIED CONSULTANT STAFF IN GRAMPIAN AND SCOTLAND 1950–80

Staff Employed by	1950	1960	1970	1980	1990[2]
(a) Health Service Grampian	56	76	106	168	(175)
(b) University of Aberdeen	9	26	37	49	(31)
(b) as % of (a+b)	14	25	25	22	(15)
(c) Health Service Scotland[1]	703	840	1315	1609	
(d) Universities of Aberdeen, Dundee, Edinburgh & Glasgow	107	147	235	278	
(d) as % of (c+d)	13	15	15	15	

1. Because of a change from 5 Regional Boards to 15 Area Boards in 1974 it is not possible to disaggregate the 4 Teaching Health Boards from all Scotland.
2. Planning Targets.

SOURCE: Scottish Health Statistics 1950–81 and University *Calendars* 1950–80

TABLE 3 SCOTTISH TEACHING AREAS WHOLE TIME EQUIVALENT MEDICAL STAFFING RATES, 1982–83

Whole Time Equiv.	Employed by		All Scot.	Grampian	Greater Glasgow	Lothian	Tayside
per £100m Annual Budget	All Medical Staff	(a) Health Service	238.7	171.0	284.9	221.9	196.4
		(b) University	30.3	35.5	22.1	47.1	17.2
		(b) as % of (a+b)	11.3	17.2	7.2	17.5	8.0

SOURCE: Scottish Health Statistics 1982–1983.

numbers of students there were changes in the form of teaching from whole class to a far greater emphasis on small groups and even individual tuition. But given due allowance for those qualitative changes, there remains a proportion of the staffing growth in excess of any increased levels of research.

Another part of the explanation can be found in Table 3, which compares medical staffing in the four Scottish Teaching Health Boards expressed as rates per £100m of budget.

Grampian had the lowest Health Service funded medical staffing of the four Scottish Teaching Boards and even with the addition of the university-funded staff still remains the lowest. These figures again imply that in Grampian the contribution of university staff to the clinical services was likely to be much greater than in the other three medical schools.

It is probable that this situation arose as an inevitable consequence of the joint developments established in the 1920s. At the start of the Health Service the Regional Board and the Court agreed to share equally the costs of the existing joint laboratory services. Despite considerable expansion of the services, the concept of such shared developments survived well into the 1970s. Indeed, in the quinquennial proposals of the medical faculty during this period many references can be found to the need for staff and resources to develop particular clinical services, and the approval of these proposals by the Court implied a continuation of the policy of shared developments. Many of these clinical initiatives took place during the period of general expansion in the university. As already indicated they were not proportionally matched by increases in undergraduate or post-graduate students, nor by an increased range of courses within the Medical School; to that extent they may represent insufficiently considered responses to demands based on a case of equity between faculties rather than academic benefits in a climate of increased resources and expansion. It was only with the escalation of Health Service costs in the latter part of the period being reviewed, when the financial allocations proposed by the Board could no longer be matched by the Court, that the policy of sharing particular costs was changed. Unfortunately this led initially to a view within the Board that the university was reneging on its responsibilities, without the Board appreciating that the funding being withdrawn had never at any time been specifically or officially earmarked for health care.

An interesting example of the implications of close involvement with clinical services arose in connection with the new laboratory block and latest extension to the Royal Infirmary known as Phase II. It had transpired at an earlier stage that if the Medical School were to be physically attached to the hospital it would be possible, within the capital costs borne by the Health Service, to incorporate certain university departments and thereby obtain new accommodation, in some instances actually embedded within the appropriate wards of the new hospital building. The clinical departments of medicine, therapeutics and surgery saw considerable advantages in such a development, and in the late sixties the protagonists and antag-onists of these proposals led faculty into the most acrimonious debates of the period, which severely damaged relationships between the clinical and para-clinical departments. It was claimed that a precedent existed because of the combined Medical Research Council/University Unit embedded in the maternity hospital. Indeed from this example it was argued, and ultimately incorporated in the plans, that the new hospital laboratories should be shared by all the clinical disciplines with, in addition, a large out-patient research clinic to encourage and ensure inter-departmental clinical research work. Other departments destined to remain in the old building argued that the move would in practice lead to less collaboration and to a break-up of the School. It certainly meant that faculty was then split into three components with the preclinical departments at Marischal College, the paraclinical departments in the Medical School and the clinical departments literally scattered throughout the hospitals at opposite ends of the Foresterhill site. In the event the new laboratories were not used as had been envisaged, few collaborative ventures were ever mounted, and the imaginative out-patient research clinic was never commissioned. What might have happened had this fragmentation not taken place is, of course, a matter of conjecture because the counter arguments of those against the scheme were never tested.

What did happen was that all three components had the opportunity to expand, albeit independently. There can be little doubt that the total physical integration of university and Health Service departments had considerable benefits for both undergraduate teaching and developments in patient care. Academic staff were on hand close to wards, students, patients and their service colleagues. Many new clinical developments arose in the resited university/Health Service combined departments, such as renal dialysis; the pulmonary laboratory; cardiac surgery; vascular surgery; renal transplantation; haematology; medical oncology; neurology; neonatology; cervical cytology; nuclear medicine; community paediatrics. It is again difficult to say whether and how these developments would have occurred had it not been for the close university involvement. Clearly a number would have occurred irrespective of the arrangements but, suffice it to say for this review, the contribution to both standards and amount of health care locally by university staff was substantial.

This close involvement had other by-products. University staff became aware of problems and short-comings in terms of service delivery and frequently initiated developments aimed at improving care and increasing effectiveness in the use of resources. From these developments arose the health information services of this area, which were considerably in advance of those in other parts of the country. Systems concerned with the integration of care between hospital and general practice also arose here and have been exported all over the world. Remodelling of psychiatric services transformed the effective use of resources. A merger of integrated care and information systems led to a patient record and monitoring system that is likely to become the basis of a new national clinical record for Scotland. Again based on records developments in Aberdeen, a prescribing and monitoring system of medical care was created which has been adopted in both hospitals and general practice and has become the progenitor of a national monitoring system and a variety of local forms of audit. Nonetheless benefits in teaching and health care have to be qualified. As services expanded, and because of the close proximity, it was convenient if some laboratories became offices and parts of the university accommodation were made available for clinical use. The intended integration of basic scientists into the clinical areas did not take place on anything approaching the scale originally envisaged. Indeed, many of the non-medical scientists associated with the clinical departments were housed in laboratories of the old medical school and the hoped for interaction between scientific staff and clinicians was therefore less than might otherwise have been achieved. Obviously there were exceptions, but frequently the new embedded laboratories served predominantly clinical rather than research needs.

A further major development of this period was the extension of clinical teaching to hospitals in Inverness. Very close links and reciprocal staff appointments have been established and along with purpose built teaching facilities there is now residential accommodation for between 30 and 40 medical undergraduates. Attachments to clinical units in Inverness during the 4th and 5th years of study have proved to be very popular and have added to the reputation of the university as an effective and committed school for medical education and practical training.

Although my contribution so far has concentrated on the provision of care to the local community by university staff, these activities were, of course, both the outcome of and the stimulus for research which, although lacking in quantity, nonetheless received national and international recognition. Outstanding examples are to be found in nuclear medicine, reproductive endocrinology, the pathogenesis of cervical cancer, social obstetrics, renal transplantation, and immunology and health services research. In virtually all the other fields smaller projects have, of course, supported and followed the clinical interests of the staff, but it would only be fair to acknowledge that for a number of the academic clinical staff at Aberdeen the predominance of their work has been on the development and provision of care rather than basic or applied medical research. These observations in turn must be set against the excellent clinical services and medical teaching in Grampian upon which many of those coming into the area as patients and students have commented so favourably.

Reviews such as this benefit enormously from hindsight, but it is worth reflecting again on the manpower figures referred to earlier. Compared to the other medical teaching centres in Scotland, Aberdeen had fewer consultants per head of the population employed directly by the Health Service. Again proportionally, there were more university employed consultants. Insidiously and over a long period major involvement of university staff in clinical work became accepted practice and in the final analysis the volume and nature of research output did not match the exceptionally high growth rate in academic staff that had taken place during the 1960s; why, how and whether such a situation arose by default is perhaps not a rewarding exercise now to pursue.

It is perhaps ironic that the greatest contribution the university Medical

School made to the region may in academic terms prove to have been its 'Achilles heel'. Much is said these days about the need for applicability and exploitability of research and the benefits of a close relationship between university disciplines and their industrial and commercial counterparts. In health care the only significant potential partner for a university is the Health Service. However in this context the activities of the Health Service appear to be considered a welfare cost rather than being seen to make a major contribution to national economic prosperity. One of the foundations of the welfare state was the belief that the health of a population was an essential portent of industrial strength. Indeed a basic requirement of the Education Acts earlier this century was that children should be healthy enough to benefit from the education to be made available. These themes reappear in the recent House of Lords Select Committee Report on Medical Research in the United Kingdom, but at present the emphasis, as far as judgements on academic research is concerned, is on the creation of knowledge rather than its application. It is unfortunate for Aberdeen that the development and application of research in clinical practice is deemed primarily a service rather than an academic function; the particularly close links of the academic clinical staff with the provision of care has led to the development and exploitation of research in practice as the major strength of the Aberdeen Medical School.

It may prove to be even more ironic as we now enter the next phase of Health Service development to which I referred earlier, namely the appropriate means of financing health care and of assessing its outcome, if the skills, experience and research programmes of the Medical School actually come into their own.

I feel I ought to end not so much with a summary as with a series of caveats. I realise that, given all the activities over the period, I have inevitably been superficial. In time, we are so close to the period being reviewed that it is difficult and invidious to single out individuals. The names of outstanding local contributors need no further testimonial from me and are to be found in numerous other records. My purpose was not to catalogue the achievements of those individuals but to identify the trends and practices of all the many people working in or with the Medical School over the past forty years and which, in turn, determined the successes and troubles of the institution as a whole. I also spent considerable time on the period before 1945 because I believe much of what has happened originated in that period and in large part pre-determined what would happen when the new link laboratories and Phase II were being planned. Thereafter while there may have been options for individuals they were fairly circumscribed and the deep rooted attitudes and expectations within the Medical School made the course that was followed well nigh inevitable.

I have had to be selective and while I have tried to be objective and relevant, I suspect that even if my selection of events has actually been appropriate my choice of qualifying adjectives may reveal a measure of my own prejudice. I believe the Medical School has served the Region well, but I fear that because of this involvement it has not served itself or the university so well. Perhaps such a judgement is too simplistic and my aggregation of events hides errors of judgement and behaviour that ought to have been identified and rectified earlier. Be that as it may, the slate now has been wiped clean—indeed if it is rubbed much more there may be no slate left. How we build, and what we build for the next phase, hopefully will benefit from this experience.

Chapter 4

Leadership within the Region

JOHN SEWELL

In the context of higher education policy the relationship between a university and its region is not unproblematic. The past chairman of the old UGC and present chief executive of the new UFC, Sir Peter Swinnerton-Dyer, has been less than sympathetic to the argument that the University of Aberdeen has a distinctive regional role, stemming from its geographical location and the social characteristics of the region it serves. Certainly the consultants employed by the university, paid for by the UGC, and reporting to both, rejected any claim that Aberdeen could argue for enhanced financial support because of its regional responsibility. That firm and consistent message has now been modified by statements made by Lord Chilver, the chairman of the UFC. During one of his forays north of the border he laid particular stress on the need for universities to develop close links with their regions. The regional relationship, especially as expressed in the response by universities to the needs of their regions, is likely to be a factor that the UFC will keep in mind during its deliberations.

Teaching and training

A university does, of course, have a number of different types of relationship with its own region. Chapter 2 analyses the impact of the university on the local labour market during the last half century. Although the strength of the local tie may be weakening, with a larger proportion of local school leavers considering universities further afield, there is little doubt that Aberdeen still retains some of the characteristics of a local university. Here there has been a tradition of producing graduates with a soundly based general education who, perhaps disproportionately, ended up in teaching. Law and medicine, although fitting into a pattern of national provision, did provide a route through which the local professions recruited.

During the 1970s the university initiated a number of postgraduate courses, with new professional opportunities in the region largely in mind. Courses in accountancy, and those in surveying provided by the department of land economy, have been particularly successful. Financial cuts since the early 1980s have resulted in a curtailment of the university's ability to provide such training. Aberdeen no longer provides a post-graduate course in clinical psychology, despite a national shortage of clinical psychologists. Social work has been rationalised to the extent that the university's department has effectively been merged with the department at Robert Gordon's Institute of Technology. But some satis-faction can be taken from the fact that the department of education escaped its threatened closure. It remains, not only as a strong research department, but also able to offer the professionally orientated M Ed.

Recently the university has moved to fill an important gap in the area of management and business studies by provision for a part-time Master's degree in Business Administration, to be mounted jointly with RGIT, with participation in planning from the Aberdeen Chamber of Commerce. This increased co-operation between RGIT and the university is evidenced not only in social work and business studies, but across a wider area including health studies, marine resources management, and rural and regional resources planning. Nationally, closer relationships between uni-versities and neighbouring polytechnics and central institutions are being actively discussed. To the extent that the demographic downturn feeds through to a decrease in the demand for higher education in the mid 1990s, the greater will be the case for closer co-operation and more efficient and effective use of resources. The first tentative step has been taken with the establishment of a joint committee, at a senior level, charged with examining areas of greater co-operation between the two institutions.

Intellectual engagement: policy and research

Another aspect of the relationship between the university and the region is in terms of intellectual engagement. There may be something of a fear that research that is rooted in the experience or 'laboratory' of the region is essentially parochial. Such a charge avoids the issue of the extent to which a university and those employed in it have a responsibility to understand, explain, and thereby give back an intellectual contribution to the locality and its people who sustain our livelihoods. Metropolitan arrogance fails to recognise the extent to which locally based research can develop concepts and methodologies and advance knowledge and have relevance to the development of a discipline nationally and internationally.

I am not competent to review the regionally grounded research that has taken place across the university; important work in, for example, literature, language, history, and the natural sciences is outside the scope of this paper. Even a survey of the work of social science departments runs the risk of giving a distorted picture by the necessity of selectivity. Over the past quarter of a century it is possible to detect a very real engagement on the part of Aberdeen social science departments with issues of public policy that were particularly relevant to the north and north east of Scotland.

Relatively early recent examples of an engagement with public policy issues can be seen both in the Gaskin Report on the future of the north-east economy and the development of the Medical Research Council's Medical Sociology Unit, following on the earlier work of Sir Dugald Baird. The policy relevance of the Gaskin Report was overtaken by the discovery and exploitation of North Sea oil, but the late 1960s and 1970s saw the economics department assessing the economic benefits to Easter Ross of the Invergordon smelter, and beginning its important work on the economic impact of North Sea oil. The restricted population base of the north-east of Scotland meant that medical sociology virtually worked itself out of a job, and the Medical Research Council transferred the unit to Glasgow.

The Highlands and Islands have continued to be a focus for policy-orientated research. The establishment of the Highlands and Islands Development Board in 1966 coincided with the expansion of the social sciences generally, and sociology in particular. Ian Carter, now professor of sociology at the University of Auckland, but originally a member of the Aberdeen sociology department, developed a radical critique of the Highland Board, and especially the theories of development which underpinned its activities. Remote, sparsely populated areas provide particular difficulties for policy makers, especially in the area of service provision. The Aberdeen department of education has conducted major studies on the provision of primary and secondary education in sparsely populated areas of northern Scotland. The interest of the Aberdeen social science departments in the problems and issues of remote rural areas led, in the mid 1970s, to the university establishing an Institute for the Study of Sparsely Populated Areas.

An area of strength that has emerged in recent years has been housing research, which has developed through research teams drawn from four different departments. Similarly, a major project on social and economic change in Aberdeen funded by the Economic and Social Research Council has involved researchers from three departments. Despite these successes there remains the feeling, largely based on responses to research project applications, that to many of those who have control over the distribution of national resources the problems and opportunities of the north and north east of Scotland are idiosyncratic and peripheral.

The university and local elites

It is appropriate in a chapter on the relationship between the university and the region to make reference to a piece of research that is at present under way and is examining the extent to which the university can be said to produce local elites. In a society where career progression and geographical mobility are often linked, and where the ownership of local companies has been increasingly internationalised, it is not necessarily to be expected that a university would produce through its own graduates members of a local elite. Indeed, the tendency for this to occur further decreases where there is a tradition of local elite families sending their sons and daughters to non-local elite universities. But if any university is likely to produce its own local elite, it can be expected to be Aberdeen. The social and geographical isolation of the city, together with its role as a traditional commercial, professional and service centre, enhances the possibility of the local production of a local elite, especially where the university has well established professional schools in medicine and law. Of course, the university's contribution to elite formation may well change over time. A change in the employment and industrial structures of the local economy may result in the displacement of locally produced elites. Similarly, an increase in geographical mobility may mean that what were primarily local labour markets take on the characteristics of national labour markets with a much wider area of geographical recruitment.

In studying elites there are two fundamentally different approaches. The reputational approach relies upon the identification of elite members by selected and well placed informants. The structural approach is based upon identifying those individuals who occupy formal positions of power, influence and social standing. The merits and limitations of both approaches constitute a continuing debate within political science. In the present study the reputational approach has been used partly because of its convenience but also because the relatively enclosed nature of Aberdeen society, and the high level of interaction among members of different elites is likely to minimise the discrepancies between reputation and reality.

The study seeks to collect information about the membership of different local elites over two time periods—1955–69 and 1970–84. The periods were deliberately selected: the earlier period is one when life in Aberdeen was untouched by North Sea oil, whereas the later period coincides with the major economic and social changes that resulted from the exploration and development of the North Sea oilfields. Throughout most of the former period Aberdeen exhibited many of the characteristics of a relatively economically disadvantaged region—low wages, a limited range of employment opportunities, and high out-migration. During much of the period the city endured poor transport links with the rest of the country. Social and geographical isolation could be expected to be relatively high. The period from 1970 to 1984 witnessed a major transformation in the economy of the city. Over the period the oil industry came to dominate the local economy. New companies, bringing with them new managers, and demanding new skills, moved into the city. The population of the area became more cosmopolitan with significant in-migration from the rest of Scotland, England, and in specific contexts from the USA, France and Holland. The growth of commuter towns around the city resulted in the neighbouring constituency of Gordon experiencing the second fastest rate of growth of all parliamentary constituencies in the United Kingdom. Transport links, especially by air, were greatly improved. The city became more explicitly integrated in a wider national and international economy and society.

The university's contribution to the production of a local elite may not only vary over time, but it may make a differential contribution across different types of elite. In the study information is being collected about seven elite areas:

1) Industry and business, including fishing and agriculture
2) Commerce and the professions
3) Political and public life
4) Local administration
5) Culture and the arts
6) Religious life
7) Education and science

The research strategy depends upon the selection of respondents who are in a position to identify elite members. This was achieved by asking a smaller group of individuals, selected on the basis of their known knowledge of those who were prominent in different areas of Aberdeen life over the two periods, to identify potential respondents. In the end 103 respondents were written to and asked to complete forms which requested information about the identity of up to ten individuals in the different areas of elite activity over the two periods. In addition, the respondents were asked to indicate whether the selected individuals were graduates of Aberdeen University. This question was included despite its possible sensitising effect. Given that respondents tended to tick the 'don't know' column for a high proportion of elite members, it would have been better to exclude the question.

The research is not at a stage where useful results can be reported. A great deal of time has been taken up with determining whether particular individuals were graduates of the university. Also, attempts are being made to increase the response rate above the present level of about a third. However, given these reservations some early observations can be made. So far the clearest finding is the extent to which the university has continued to produce elite members in the area of the professions, reflecting the dominance of local firms and local families in law, and to a lesser extent in medicine. In the area of business and industry, the respondents declined to identify as elite members oil company managers and executives who may have had a limited period of residence in Aberdeen, but who during that time exercised considerable control over the economic fortunes of the city. Even so, graduates of the university do not appear to be well represented among the business and industrial elite. In contrast, Aberdeen graduates may have strengthened their elite representation between the two periods in the areas of education and science, and arts and culture.

The area that emerges in both periods as being least penetrated by local graduates at elite level is that of political and public life. In part, this is because of the early control that the trades union and Labour movements exercised over local municipal politics. A university that produced a professional elite failed to penetrate a political elite that was predominantly Labour and working class. The only name of anyone connected with the university that appears in the earlier period is that of Lord Provost Graham, a professor of theology who became a Labour town councillor. In the later period, the representation of Aberdeen graduates is just as sparse, but there emerges, at the time of local government reorganisation, a group of university academic employees who were active in municipal politics. Despite achieving formal positions of power and influence, they should perhaps be seen as an aberration whose influence had disappeared within a decade of the 1974 local government reorganisation.

If the present study can be satisfactorily concluded it will enable us to understand the extent to which the university produced a local elite during a period when the social and economic base of the city and the region was undergoing fundamental restructuring.

Conclusion

In terms of providing highly qualified and trained entrants to the local labour market, the university has a well developed regional role. If the university is to thrive rather than survive, it is likely that we are going to be encouraged to be even more sensitive to the needs of the region. Such a development will affect what we teach, what we research, and our relationship with industry. But the activity of a university cannot be determined purely by reference to commercial criteria and interests. A university must retain a public service responsibility. We have a critical and questioning function to perform and to that extent the aims and objectives of the university must not be distorted by an understandable desire to take advantage of market opportunities.

Chapter 5

The Student Experience, 1945–1978

COLIN McLAREN

This is an account of student life outside the lecture room, told where possible in the words of the students themselves. They are drawn from the student publications *Gaudie* and *Alma Mater*; from 'Notes' on undergraduate affairs in the *Aberdeen University Review*; and from contributions to the university's Oral History Project.

Gaudie, the student newspaper, alone covers the whole period. Struggling to reconcile its functions as an organ of the Students' Representative Council, a channel of hard news and a forum for opinion, it is strident, flatulent—and often perceptive. *Alma Mater*, once a forum, was by 1945 essentially a literary magazine: 'For the past few years', said the editor in 1950, '[it] has consisted almost entirely of the work of the Honours English School'. It carried several features on student life, however, before expiring in the 1960s. The Notes in the *Review* are sometimes brief chronicles, sometimes sharp commentaries by former student officials; the last appeared in 1964.

The Oral History Project (OHP) has hitherto concentrated on the pre-war generations but interviews have been recorded with post-war students when the chance has arisen and these have been augmented by written reminiscences. There are as a result some thirty memoirs of student life from 1945 to 1965: too few for analysis, but enough to provide illustrations.

Alumni of the 1940s who contributed to the project were almost all first-generation students for whom a university education had, nevertheless, seemed a natural progression: 'it was more or less assumed', said one. ' "Sandy's brilliant, he'll go to university" ' (MA 1950, PhD 1954). For those from the North East, the choice of Aberdeen was almost automatic, encouraged by the bursary system and the expectation of many parents that their children would study at or near home: 'In my time, it would have been most unusual not to go to the local university...' (MA 1951).

Some contributors were wholly supported by their families: 'My father financed me entirely. I had no help from anywhere else at all and I'm grateful to him for it. [I had] five shillings a week for personal spending; everything else was budgeted out. I don't remember feeling very short of money' (MA 1947). Others lived on permutations of bursaries, grants and earnings: 'I had a county bursary of some sort plus the usual Carnegie [grant towards fees] plus a local scholarship plus what my parents could contribute. In addition to that, I worked every summer on the farm. I had to, really, to make ends meet' (MA 1951). Those whose careers had been interrupted by war service received government Grants for Further Education and Training.

Just over half of the student population lived at home, the rest in lodgings. The quality of lodgings and landladies varied. 'I lived in two sets, firstly in Hilton Avenue, latterly in Brighton Place. Both honest-to-goodness Aberdeen landladies ... [One] must have been over seventy but she brooded over ... two policemen, two excisemen and two or sometimes three students ... She charged 35 shillings a week which I suppose was just below the standard for the time. We were well fed on porridge and stovies and other wholesome fare ...' (BSc 1952). 'I remember the cold, because, of course, there was no central heating or anything like that. You were rather restricted and you had to be in by certain times. Landladies were fairly tough in those days' (MA 1952).

Based at home or in 'digs', students were largely dependent on the university for company and recreation. The facilities available were described in *Regent*, a handbook published by the SRC for new students. The first issue (1948) introduced them to the SRC, the Union, the Debater and the Athletics Association; to the lodgings registry and the newly-founded medical service; to the Chapel and the gymnasium; to the training corps and the air squadron; and to 'University Music'. In addition, it listed 29 societies: 13 were subject-based, four (the Elphinstone, the Evangelical, the Episcopal and the Student Christian Movement) were religious; three (the Scottish Nationalist, the Socialist and the Unionist) were political; the rest were cultural and recreational, including the Mermaid (play-reading) and the Lairig (hill-walking). There were also 14 sports clubs.

The Union, its membership mixed (unique among Scottish universities), was the principal resort. The Auld Toon Cafe and some city bars were traditionally popular—one advertised itself as 'the place where students meet'. And there were other haunts: 'The societies only went on till about half past nine; then you would try and find somewhere where you could have a cup of coffee. There were these sort of Italian coffee-ice-cream places. You got absolutely appalling coffee but nevertheless we stuck it out and we drank our coffee and we would talk. We would talk enormously' (MA 1950, PhD 1954).

Friendships often derived from a shared background; just as often they transcended it. 'My friends tended to come from Highland circles', said a contributor from Skye, who met them in the Celtic Society and the Shinty Club, 'but in fact my best friend was from Fraserburgh' (BSc 1952). Money, or the lack of it, was not a barrier; nor were class and gender. According to one contributor, however, choice of faculty could be: 'We lived such a very insulated life at King's. We all knew each other very, very well, spent four years in this small group. We didn't really mix an awful lot' (MA 1952).

Relations between senior staff and students were as formal outside the lecture room as they were within it. 'Some GIs were on the course and they rushed up one day with cameras and said, "Say, hold it, professor", taking photographs with a flash camera—and we were appalled!' (MA 1947). A few contributors recalled tea parties with professors or the principal: 'We all were on our best behaviour and we wore very respectable clothes. All the men wore white shirts and dark ties. We shook hands and spoke in very low voices' (MA 1952).

Relations with lecturers and assistants were easier. They might be encountered over lunch in the Elphinstone Hall refectory and sometimes in the evening: 'Dr Barber [German] used to invite us round for beer and sandwiches and chat ... I don't think we had close contacts with any of the others' (MA 1951). In a small department, an older student might fraternise with junior staff of almost the same age: 'Socially, we were on Christian-name terms', said one (BSc 1950), adding that the student-lecturer relationship was always resumed in class.

The Note in the *Review* of Summer 1946 claimed that student life had acquired a fresh vigour. 'There were "Golden Days" soon after the 1914–18 war and ... there will be golden days of a sort again before so very long.' Like others, the writer was relying upon returning ex-servicemen and women to provide them.

The university's statistical returns do not give precise numbers of those who returned. In 1946–7, however, almost a third of the students received FET grants; the proportion rose substantially in 1948–9 but had fallen the following year to about a quarter. It was assumed, not unreasonably, that student life would benefit from their age and experience. When the expectation was not at first fulfilled, the tone of the Notes grew reproachful: 'For some time now, there has been a hope that the ex-Servicemen would be a stimulant for our war-jaded "Alma Mater". Unfortunately, most of them have pledged their vitality to other women, and are inextricably involved in the "diplomaniac" hurdy-gurdy' (Spring 1948).

'I think the ex-service students were very much more serious than the younger students', one of them told the OHP. 'We really knew what we wanted to do. When we were working, we worked very hard. When we weren't working, we enjoyed ourselves'. Enjoyment meant the Union hops, dances in the Mitchell Hall and membership of the departmental society. 'I really wasn't interested in the student politics or anything of that sort' (BSc 1950).

Nevertheless, a number did participate actively in student affairs. 'They tended to run everything', said a contributor, 'the publications and the newspapers and the entertainments' (MA 1952). She found their presence stimulating, a view which others shared: 'There was I at sixteen, and some of my closest friends were probably about twenty-eight. ... I think that there might have been some people who rather avoided the company of the older ones. I found myself drawn to them because I felt they had something to offer and they treated me like an equal' (MA 1950, Ph D 1954).

In 1950, as the influx of ex-servicemen diminished, *Alma Mater* carried two assessments of their impact. The first, by Peter Blacklaws, claimed that their influence 'has been almost wholly unfortunate'. Some had 'presided over Councils, Committees and coffee-tables', inhibiting younger students from participating. Others had spread 'warped conceptions of education which have manifested themselves in the aggressive denigration of anything that smacks of culture'. The second, unsigned, agreed that a few 'had elected to carry the banner for aggressive Philistinism'. But the writer claimed that the presence of older men had been generally beneficial to students straight from school and regretted only that it had not succeeded in breaking down further the barriers between students and staff.

During the first six years of the 1950s, the student population crept towards 2,000. In 1950 four out of ten came from Aberdeen itself, four from the surrounding counties, one from the rest of Scotland and one from England or abroad. Students living in lodgings gradually outnumbered those living at home. 'A major question of policy engaging the university', said Principal Taylor, was the provision of halls of residence (*Review*, Spring 1950).

The first of the halls in Old Aberdeen (there was already provision for the Medical School at Foresterhill) was not opened until the end of the decade. In the meantime, the university and the SRC tried to resolve problems which the growth in numbers had created. Lecturers meeting in the Inter-Faculty Group learned of 'a real feeling of bewilderment during the first year' (*Review*, Spring 1954). The appointment of staff as 'regents', from 1953, was one attempt to reduce it. The SRC had committees on welfare, the registration of lodgings and the provision of books.

Its operations grew with the decade and it was commended in the *Review* (Spring 1958) for its involvement with 'travel, employments, grants, the Scottish Union of Students and general welfare'.

Pressure of numbers was also a problem for the Union Management Committee, highlighted in the *Review* of Spring 1956: 'The Union, designed to accommodate the leisure hours of some 500 students, now strives to cope with the patronage of some 1,500 of the Undergraduates and Staff, who chiefly make use of its dining and snack-bar facilities.' Moreover, its very nature was threatened by the proposed hall and the movement of departments to Old Aberdeen. 'We must cease to regard it as a cheap eating-house alone. We must seek to preserve its unity as a meeting place.'

The problem for the Debater was not so much numbers as a lack of them. Much of the decade was spent in efforts—'Dining Hall Debates and Public Occasions' was how they were dismissed in the *Review* (Spring 1953)—to attract better speakers and bigger audiences.

There were rectorials in 1951 and 1954. The first, won by comedian Jimmy Edwards from a field which included the black singer Paul Robeson, raised serious questions about the nature of the rectorship; the second was notorious for a display of excessive force by the police. Add to this a resurgence in student drama and the emergence of new societies (for Humanism, Liberalism, and the Study of Contemporary European Literature) and it is clear that in the first six years of the decade there was abundant scope for student activity.

The value of participation was emphasised to new entrants, as a contributor to the OHP recalled: 'There was a Preterminal Gathering weekend which included ... a lecture on how to be a student by Rex Knight, the Psychology Professor. We should work five nights a week, he said, and join three societies, one related to work, one of general interest, and one physically active' (BSc 1956).

Further encouragement came from junior staff, as another contributor remembered: 'We had an unusually brilliant collection of young lecturers who were passing through'. From a cosmopolitan background, she eagerly joined the group that formed around Denys Munby [political economy]. 'We met for about a year or two and talked about [philosophy], religion and politics: and really anything anyone wanted to talk about; and it was rather marvellous because on the whole I found Scottish students rather reserved.' Not surprisingly, perhaps, she was active in the SRC and student politics. 'There was the Robeson Committee—which, in fact, was the Labour Group; and, of course, Peace with China, which was a mixed, Popular Front thing. But I think it was actually a very tiny proportion— the same, I don't know, hundred students—who did all these things. ... There was a Scottish Nationalist Group too, and I remember—perhaps I just liked marching—I remember marching with them down Union Street too.' (MA 1952).

The other contributors took part in social, recreational and religious activities, rattled cans in the Charities campaign, and sang in the Student Show; but they were less concerned with politics: 'I joined Scottish Country Dancing which only lasted a year, some scientific society of which I have no recollection, and the SCM, which became my main interest. ... War on Want came into being about then so we tried to persuade all our acquaintances to join us in giving up coffee and donating the money instead. ... None of us read a newspaper beyond the [Aberdeen] *Press and Journal* and then only for local news; we were supremely uninterested in party politics despite the urgings of our SCM elders and betters' (BSc 1956).

Although there were opportunities for participation and evidence that students took them, the recurrent theme in student writing and reportage of the period is the prevalence of apathy. According to *Gaudie* (26 January 1950): 'undergraduate life is being run by about ten to twelve individuals, who, willy-nilly, are thrust into a multiplicity of activities out of all proportion to their best interests, and, in many cases, their own personal desires'. The Note in the *Review* of that year ended grimly: 'Many would say that there is a spirit of fearfulness abroad, and a submerging of free, vigorous, independent and original thought—which should be the special characteristic of a University Student Body—and its replacement by mediocrity, convention for its own sake, and staid dullness'.

The subject resurfaced in a series of trenchant Notes by David Craig between 1951 and 1953. He accepted that a degree of apathy was inevitable. It was possible, he wrote, 'that our fluid Scottish non-residential university has always relied upon the virile individual growth on the solid substratum of duller clay. It seems unlikely that undergraduate writing and debating would flourish more because of greater social-university consciousness'. Nevertheless, he perceived the danger that arose when the nucleus of active students was too small: 'the mass turns upon it as an officious coterie; and we find, for example, that office-holding students are looked on as petty tyrants or ambitious egotists'. He was, throughout, bitterly critical of the intellectual unadventurousness of most students: 'of the two literary societies, the Mermaid has succeeded this term [Winter 1952] with big attendances, and the Lit. has failed ...: note that the Mermaid is a reading-group whose material is ready made, the Lit. a discussion group whose impulse can come only from the independent minds of its members'.

Pegged to events in the terms he covered—the 'Crusade for the Toga' of 1951, for example, the Edwards rectorial, the Peace with China Committee and the controversial Pacifist Society—Craig's account of the ebb and flow of apathy in the student body is inevitably disjointed. A more coherent assessment, by Brian Mitchell and Charles Thomson, appeared in *Alma Mater* (April 1952). It was based on a survey of students serving on the SRC, UMC and the committees of societies and clubs. 'The total of 367 ... out of 1,900 shows that apathy is not so great as has sometimes been suggested. ... On the other hand, a figure of less than one active student in five does not indicate an exceptionally flourishing undergraduate society.' In fact, when departmental societies were excluded, the number involved fell to one in seven.

Of particular significance was the relative inactivity of students from the North and North-East, especially from the counties. It was attributed to a traditional austerity of character; to differences in education, notably the failure of country schools to prepare their pupils for the non-academic aspects of university life; and to the fact that many local students, coming from lower income groups, felt obliged to concentrate on their work or believed that they had not enough money to participate in the non-academic side. The stimulus of joining a new community in a new region, a factor in explaining the involvement of students from the south, evidently left those from the north unaffected.

The Note of Spring 1954, while recording criticisms of student apathy, suggested that the distractions should not be disparaged: 'a home life and a country community more part of ourselves, as honestly worthy, and certainly more wholly vital and satisfactory than any university can hope to be'. That of the following year took an equally strong line: 'it is largely student awareness and not apathy which accounts for the success or failure of society evenings, since the student knows that they are inevitably dull'.

'Then, suddenly, dramatically, the atmosphere was changed' (*Review*, Spring 1957). Suez provoked a crowded and bitter contest in the Debater and some 800 students, meeting in the Mitchell Hall, protested against Soviet intervention in Hungary. 'Suez and Hungary', declared James Burns, lecturer in politics and a stern critic of student apathy, 'have drawn from the Aberdeen students a display of political concern far surpassing anything in the past decade or more' (*Gaudie*, 16 November 1956).

It was short-lived. The Note for Autumn is bitter: 'Honour was served, the conscience of Humanity and of Aberdeen University students was summarily appeased'. Subsequent fund-raising efforts for Hungarian students, the writer claimed, had been ill-organised and unsupported. 'Had not the UMC with characteristic largesse donated about £100 ... the present tally of about £300 would have been farcical instead of just ironic.' Written reminiscences contributed to the OHP refer to the two episodes but add few details. One comment, however, echoes the note of anti-climax: 'The only world event I remember was the Hungarian Uprising because some of our boys were talking of going to join it but they never did' (MA 1958).

Together, however, the events revitalised the Debater for a time and planted a thin, tough strain of political awareness in the student community. 'At the time of my arrival ... recollections were still vivid of the Suez and Hungarian crises ... and out of these had emerged the New Left Movement. I made its acquaintance because someone had arranged for its journals to be on sale in the coffee shop in the Elphinstone Hall, but shortly after an Aberdeen club was formed, the majority of whose members were from the university' (MA 1962).

Early in the 1960s, as the university began to accelerate towards a population of 6,000, Angus MacIntyre considered the implications in *Alma Mater* (Spring 1961): 'Aberdeen is to undergo such a change within the next ten years that many of the traditional facets of our existence will be destroyed whilst others are likely to be so altered as to make recognition of what went before difficult, if not impossible'.

The university strove to retain a human face. The regenting system, for example, was replaced in 1966 by a more elaborate scheme of regents and advisers. The SRC, too, struggled to keep pace with the changes. 'For the first time the Council has been consulted by the authorities on problems of expansion. ... Its regular work has been facilitated by an increase in the number of Faculty representatives, a very necessary step in view of the greater demand for the various services offered to students. ... There is a growing appreciation of such facilities as Travel Employments, Tutorial, Insurances etc.' (*Review*, Spring 1964).

The successful integration of the new population depended to a large extent on the character of the new hall of residence, Crombie, and of those that were to follow. MacIntyre's first impression was favourable but cautious: 'If [the others] are merely additional sleeping blocks, the value of Crombie Hall, as it is now, will decline'. Not everyone shared his view of the hall, however: 'There is a general feeling that the inmates, as they are called, have developed into a pseudo-sophisticated elite, disdaining to have any contact with less fortunate students who still "rough it" in lodgings' (*Review*, Spring 1961).

None of the OHP's contributors from the 1960s lived in hall; most of them were in lodgings. As accommodation grew scarcer and landlords more astute, 'roughing it' was in some cases not an over-statement. 'I had an attic room with breakfast and evening meal for which I paid £2.10s. a week. As my total weekly income was £3 I didn't often eat lunch, though I do remember an occasional warm, flakey morning-roll in the Union' (MA 1962). 'I lived in the following streets, which seemed to be popular with other students: Rosemount Place, Dee Street, Polmuir Road, Calsayseat Road and Irvine Place. ... Only two were completely satisfactory. Some were very poor—we were cold and damp, food was insufficient or of indifferent quality and bathroom facilities restricted' (MA

1965). Early in the decade, however, the preference for independence was apparent: 'More and more students are seeking complete freedom to live their own lives ... they are living, or wanting to live, in flats' (*Gaudie*, 13 November 1963).

Cheap lunches at the increasingly crowded Union or the Elphinstone Hall were supplemented by fish and chips from 'a small shop which had somehow managed to escape the attention of the public health authorities' (MA 1965). 'Then the first Chinese restaurant came to Aberdeen—2*s*. 6*d*. for a 3-course lunch, always an English dish included for suspicious locals. This led to a much wider choice of cheap eating-places.' (MA 1962).

If expansion led to outsized classes and overcrowded facilities, it also promoted an upsurge in student activities, which was reported with enthusiasm in the *Review*. Participation by first-year students and by women increased: at one debate 'six women spoke from the floor, an event hitherto unheard of. ... Furthermore the editor of *Gaudie* for the past two terms has been a woman'. The newspaper itself was praised: 'Enthusiasm for [it] has rocketed, and sales have trebled, so that it is now the largest-selling student paper in the country'. In drama, plays by (predictably) Ionesco, Osborne and Anouilh were interspersed with the work of student writers; while a production in-the-round by Reginald Barrett-Ayres [music] to mark the Shakespeare Quatercentenary was 'the result of massive effort by many student societies and is as much an indication of the enthusiasm of the University in 1964 as anything can be'.

A performance of Giraudoux's *Tiger at the Gates*, said a Note of Spring 1962, 'no doubt appealed to the growing armies in the University sporting little black and white badges'. The Campaign for Nuclear Disarmament had a considerable impact. An exhibition in a hall near the Union immediately converted one of the OHP's contributors (MA 1962). 'Friends appeared in perpetual black', said another, 'and sounded moral' (MA 1962). The student branch recorded in *Regent* (1960) that its members had marched to Aldermaston and Glasgow, and along Union Street and had shown a film of Hiroshima. By 1965, however, wearing black and sounding moral was not enough. Criticised by *Gaudie* for their involvement with activists of the local Youth CND, the chairman of the student branch retorted: 'There is a growing body of opinion within the peace movement which considers that ... a hostile public is rather preferable to an apathetic one: people are at least made to think' (*Gaudie*, 10 November 1965). Soon afterwards, two members of the student branch raided a civil defence centre.

Apartheid was also the object of organised protest. In 1964 over 800 students packed the Union for a meeting which imposed a boycott on South African goods there. 'It raised quite heated feelings', a contributor to the OHP recalled, 'particularly from those who felt banning South

African produce was a trivial gesture; [there was] the feeling that the Union was being used by political activists to ride their own political hobby horses' (BSc 1965).

Contributions to the OHP and comment in the *Review* come to an end in 1965. For impressions of student life in the second half of the decade, culminating in the years of Student Revolt, the principal source is *Gaudie*. In the absence of other evidence, however, it is difficult to say how far the campaigns and controversies reported and publicised in its columns reflect the opinions and aspirations of the student body as a whole.

In 1967 mass demonstrations against increased fees for overseas students marked the beginning of campus insurgency in Britain (Alexander Cockburn and Robin Blackburn, *Student Power*, London, 1969). There was little opposition in Aberdeen, however, where the intake of overseas students was comparatively low. In 1968 protests at the government's decision not to raise student grants were likewise poorly supported. A mass meeting— the first in a decade—was called: 'Instead of the massive show of force the SRC needed ... all they got was a very half-hearted attempt to condemn the Government's policy from a small part of the student body'. Those who stayed away 'were quite satisfied with the grants situation as it now stands' (*Gaudie*, 14 February 1968).

In contrast, a prolonged campaign for the publication of departmental failure rates arose from what seems to have been general concern over methods of teaching and examining in the expanded university. Beginning in 1966, it reached a climax in November 1968 when a call by the president of the SRC for direct action was followed by a brief occupation of the Registry. *Gaudie*, which had supported the campaign while distancing itself from the activists, played down the militancy of the event but conceded its success: 'As a result of their action, there took place perhaps the largest ever mass meeting of Aberdeen students at which the Principal undertook to supply failure rates within seven days. ... While this action was as spontaneous as any "revolution" can be, the danger is that in the future such enthusiasm may be turned to the wrong ends by people who care less about issues concerning students, and more about corruption and chaos' (13 November 1968).

The warning proved unnecessary. Although the shrill rhetoric of the Left continued undiminished, campaigns for participation in academic affairs and representation in university government were conducted by deliberation and consultation, notably through the University Committee with representatives from Court, Senatus and the SRC. The process was strengthened by the election as rector of Jo Grimond, who appointed as his assessor on Court the secretary of the SRC. The choice of Grimond in preference to the radical Robin Blackburn and the unpredictable Clement Freud, was taken by *Gaudie* 'as a sign from students of their (perhaps strained) willingness to continue working within a modified version of the present framework' (3 December 1969).

Minor controversies, often over the regulations of the halls of residence, seem to have raised little interest among students at large. *Gaudie* itself grew exasperated: 'For the most part the inmates of Halls are a peaceful crowd who cannot really be bothered with the petty politics of the few who like to make out that Hall-life can be equated with prison-life' (31 January 1968).

The extent of student interest in national and international affairs is harder to assess. There were teach-ins on comprehensive education and world population (1966), drugs and Ulster (1969). *Gaudie* dutifully published reports on Rhodesia, Vietnam and Czechoslovakia. But hopes that the Debater would become 'a sort of *24 Hours* studio in the flesh where issues [Vietnam, Nigeria, labour disputes] are thrashed out, both between key people at the centre of them and interested students and staff' (*Gaudie*, 25 October 1967) were unfulfilled. Vietnam alone was the subject of sustained action. Following the collaboration between the student and city CND in 1965, students became active in the Aberdeen Committee for Peace in Vietnam. A feature in *Gaudie* implied that the core of protesters was small but reported that there was general support from religious and political societies in the university (10 May 1968).

During the 1970s the possibility of further expansion and its effect upon the quality of student life inside and outside the lecture room, was a source of considerable disquiet to students and their representatives. The size of the university and its increasing impersonality were already causing distress. 'Loneliness', said the Student Progress Officer, 'is the greatest problem we have to face' (*Gaudie*, 13 February 1974).

Appointed in 1970 in direct response to the agitation over failure rates, she joined a 'welfare net' comprising the chaplains, the Student Health Service, wardens, regents and advisers, and remained part of it until 1974. In 1975 an enquiry by the SRC into the effectiveness of the system produced praise for Student Health, criticisms of regents and advisers, and a paradox: 'The main single source of advice on non-academic matters was members of teaching staff not specifically related to Student Welfare. Students ... get to know the staff first through academic work and only then choose who to approach from a personal angle' (*Gaudie*, 26 November 1975). Regenting was subsequently eliminated, except in the science faculty, but the network was reinforced when the SRC established a branch of the student support service, Niteline: 'Usually we find that listening is all that people want us to do' (*Gaudie*, 22 October 1975).

It was not just the lonely who needed to talk. In 1971 the mental health department surveyed the sexual behaviour and contraceptive practice of women students: 'The opportunity to give vent to these topics would seem to have been welcomed. Many of the replies contained pleas for improved arrangements for obtaining contraceptive advice and criticisms of the present facilities' (*BMJ*, 1972). By 1975, however, the Student Health Service was able to tell *Gaudie* of a steady increase in advice on contraception.

The predicament of homosexuals in the student community was also first publicised in 1971: 'Is it too much to ask for something a little better than the awkward chat with the Chaplaincy Centre or Student Health?' an anonymous correspondent demanded in *Gaudie* (7 January). A branch of the Scottish Minorities Group was founded in the following year, but it was not until 1975 that Gaysoc was established. By 1978 it had opened a Gay Switchboard and reported the emergence of a gay community in the city.

There was concern, too, over sexual equality and sexism. Women's Liberation held its first meeting in the university in 1971. Sexist lapses in *Gaudie* were vigorously rebuked: 'Could you explain why racism is so abhorrent that we occupy [the administration building] over it, while sexism is fostered and encouraged in our own "newspaper"...' (16 November 1977). In 1979 women students, angry at sexual harassment and attacks, staged a march to 'reclaim the night'.

A prevalent and persistent cause of anxiety was the shortage of accommodation. The number of places in halls of residence had been increased by the extensive development at Hillhead, and the halls themselves had lost their elite image: 'The main advantage is the privacy of your own warm room, which allows you to work when you please and bring friends in' (*Gaudie*, 26 January 1972). Nevertheless, many students preferred to share flats in the city, and found themselves competing unsuccessfully against workers in the oil industry. *Gaudie* regularly carried stories of substandard facilities, ruthless landlords and exploited students. The SRC established a service to advise tenants of their rights and to mediate in disputes. Its caseload was lessened by the provisions of the Rent Act of 1974, but these in turn discouraged landlords from letting to students, and for a time the shortage grew worse.

The existence of distress cannot be ignored, but it should not be exaggerated. For most students, life outside the lecture room was doubtless as agreeable in the 1970s as in earlier decades, each session culminating in the uninhibited festivities of the Charities Campaign and the frolics of the Student Show. There was no lack of meeting places in the university, although the need for a new Union building was frequently reiterated. A report on catering facilities (*Gaudie*, 9 May 1973) suggests that they were adequate if unenticing. The Central Refectory (replacing the Elphinstone Hall) in Old Aberdeen was 'as plastic as it ever was but the plastic sure is grubby now'; and the Pavilion 'reminds one of a work camp'. The waitress service at the Union 'gives it an air of respectability', but the reporter's evident preference was for city cafes and bars.

Opportunities to participate in student activities were more plentiful than ever, with the establishment of groups dedicated to voluntary work for the less-privileged. 'Anyone left cold after that lot', said an ebullient Fresher, reviewing Societies Morning for *Gaudie* in 1970, 'must be very hard to please.' *Gaudie* claimed that many were: 'It is the same dedicated band of students (mainly of the left) who are in charge of the political societies, run the Debater, attend the debates, organise the sit-ins, sit in, and form the large part of the standard sub-quorum audiences at any of the SRC's mass meetings. ... Altogether this group numbers about two hundred...' Castigating the lack of commitment to voluntary work— plenty ate the bread-and-cheese lunches: not enough painted the walls— the editor turned to the societies: 'audiences may go to thirty—with a bit of luck' (1 October 1970).

In student politics, the choice of two media-men and an actor as rectors during the decade suggests that the enthusiasm of the late 1960s had, indeed, evaporated. Nevertheless, some issues did provoke a wide and forceful response. In 1971 a 'day of action', protesting at threats to the funding of student unions, included an almost total boycott of lectures and what the SRC *Report* called 'a rather aimless march of about 3,000'. In 1973 there was a demonstration for higher grants. 'Be on the march', *Gaudie* exhorted its readers: some 2,000 from the university and the city colleges responded.

The most dramatic episode of the decade was in protest at apartheid. In 1973 the SRC made representations to the university on its investment in firms with South African subsidiaries. These were renewed in 1976 and in October 1977 students occupied the administration building for two weeks. The confrontation was generally peaceful: damage was limited to a broken hinge and a stained seat. Although the issue of disinvestment remained unresolved, it is clear from correspondence in *Gaudie* that the action itself prompted considerable debate amongst students, fanned by the inevitable flurry of leaflets: 40–45,000 sheets of paper were used (*Gaudie*, 9 November 1977). 'Throughout the session', the SRC reported, 'the attention of the student body to SRC and university affairs remained higher than anything seen in recent years.'

In contrast, commitment to the less privileged improved little over the decade, as *Gaudie* complained in 1978. A feature emphasised the value of voluntary work—'probably the best way to break out from the island of indifference that student life tends to promote'—but calculated that 'if all the active members of all the social concern societies are added together, they make up only a few hundred...' Confirmation of this estimate appeared in the reports that followed: the Simon Society (helping the single homeless) had 20 members from the university and city colleges; Amnesty International had 25 active members in the university but support from around 100; Friends of the Earth had 100; Niteline, 28; Women's Action Group, 50. No figures were recorded for Third World First and Task Force (29 November 1978).

Student apathy was thus as much a cause of comment and concern in 1978 as it had been thirty years before. But whereas an explanation of its earlier manifestations could be attempted, the inadequacy of the evidence for the 1960s and 1970s makes such an exercise impractical. Apathy is, indeed, only one of several issues from these decades which await further investigation; not least among them what Robert Anderson calls the shift from student life to student culture (*THES*, 3 March 1989). The student community, from the mid 1960s onwards, has grown increasingly complex: it is diverse in origin and split between home, hall, bed-sitter and flat. It cannot be studied merely from the columns of *Gaudie*, the minutes of the SRC, or leaflets of the Left and Right. There is, in short, an urgent need for the recollections of alumni of the period, those who were active in student affairs and, no less important, those who were not.

Commentary to Chapter 5

Voices from Three Generations

1. COLIN MACLEAN (Faculty of Arts, 1942–3, 1947–50)

My student experience began in 1942. I left Robert Gordon's College at
the end of fifth year to grab a year at university before being called up. I
left Gordon's in early June to spend a long summer driving the food van
and operating the telephone exchange at the Royal Mental Hospital,
Cornhill: the van driver had been called up. Having been in the Gordon's
Air Training Corps, I joined the University Air Squadron, which occupied
a lot of weekend and some weekday time. I firewatched at King's—every
sixth night, I think. It was not possible to be a solitary student.

I greatly enjoyed that first year at university, and in my four years
(grounded after changed eyesight requirements) as a radar mechanic at the
back and bottom of the Royal Air Force, my principal aim in life was to
return to university, which I did in time to begin the 1947–8 session.

Not given to nostalgia—or, as it happens, to regrets—I have never
wished to return to student life, but I have never been happier than I was
in my four years at Aberdeen University. I had hated school. My university
years were full years. As I remember, the term 'active student' was common then for the student who did something more than merely attend
classes. Perhaps I qualified as hyperactive and should therefore be seen as
atypical.

My Honours English course, typical of many at that time, was supported
by Ordinary passes in Latin, philosophy, French and history, the first three
of these belonging to the categories of required options. I was for one
session (1948–9) editor of *Gaudie* (in which session the student population
rose above 2,000 for the first time). I originated and organised the successful
campaign to make Lord Tweedsmuir rector in 1948. I took part in turn
as performer, administrator, author and composer (i.e. of tunes) in five
Charity Week Shows at His Majesty's Theatre, being wholly responsible,
after graduation, for book and lyrics of the 1951 Show *Spring in Your
Step*. I was involved in the Debater, not then a focus of much student

interest or activity. I do not remember missing any lectures, I passed all my examinations and excelled in none. Like most ex-servicemen I knew, I spent all of the summer holidays in employment—in my case, back in the Mental Hospital.

During term I was frequently in the Union. I attended Saturday hops— and Sunday Chapel the next morning—regularly. Our quickstepping, and quick-birling, at hops sometimes attained high velocity, especially to 'Twelfth Street Rag'. Other melodies still echoing from those years are 'Music, Music, Music' (made popular by Richard Attenborough in a weekend record programme on the wireless), 'Almost Like Being in Love', 'People Will Say We're in Love', 'Nancy with the Laughing Face' (one of the few records in the tannoy library on the Castle Line troopship from Malta to Southampton in 1947) and 'If I Knew You Were Coming I'd Have Baked a Cake'—this when mothers and landladies took personal pride in being able to assemble the necessary ingredients.

Quite different music was to be heard at Chapel and at the recitals under Willan Swainson, by then head of the new music department, whose only full-time member of staff was the assistant lecturer Edward Downes (now a conductor of world repute). Downes wished to stage *The Marriage of Figaro*. Swainson disapproved, because the story was improper—he would have tolerated *Fidelio*. Swainson also declined to play the Wedding March in King's Chapel at weddings. My guess is that Principal Taylor would have supported these fastidious rulings. *Figaro* was staged in the Union, not under university or music department auspices, and was counted a success. Downes had strong Communist leanings and refused to have 'The King' played, as was then the custom, before curtain-up. My friend, George Sinclair, then on the SRC, tried but failed to have Downes instructed to play 'The King'. We compensated Sinclair by singing 'The King' as he mounted the platform later that year at his graduation.

Sinclair, too, played some part—by removing the appropriate keys— in ensuring that King's Crown Tower was for part of one day accessible only to members of the Tweedsmuir campaign: this was the morning after a Tweedsmuir banner had been wrapped round the Crown. Tweedsmuir supporters also tackled the Mitchell Tower. These were mountaineering medicals: it was necessary to recruit students from all faculties to a rectorial campaign committee. Even so, we only narrowly defeated the Malcolm Sargent team. For the rectorial fight in Marischal Quad the Tweedsmuir ammunition was mainly fish-heads rolled in soot. Tweedsmuir stood the campaign group a remarkable sherry party somewhere in Market Street— my memory of it is sweet but vague.

By far the best opportunity for inter-faculty friendships was the Student Show, then a grouping fairly distinct from the Dramatic Society, which excelled around then in its production of Webster's *The White Devil*

(1948). There were tensions as well as friendships—and, of course, sudden romances—in Shows. Some thought that Shows should be more daring and innovative—Shows were neither. Others, of whom I was one, thought Shows should give priority to raising money and therefore to maintaining the large, regular audiences they then attracted, not least with an appreciable number of sketches or characters presented in broad Doric. (Buff Hardie, now of *Scotland the What?*, tells me he spoke his first line on stage in *Spring in Your Step*). These shows were pre-television, often markedly derivative in content, but they made money, they were great fun, and also they effectively mixed not only the sexes and the faculties but also the age-groups—i.e. the ex-servicemen and those straight from school. In those years, too, there was (for peace-time) an unprecedented number of students from outwith the university's traditional catchment areas, some of them men who had been at the university during the war on short-service courses.

The ex-servicemen (and some ex-servicewomen) could be distinguished partly by their age, sometimes by their dress—for items of uniform were useful supplements to the demob issue—but seldom, as I recall, by any tendency to talk war. We knew remarkably little about one another's service careers. I think one student was said to have had a South Atlantic island named after him because of some naval exploit. But I think I have, in the late 1980s, heard more reminiscing about wartime experience than I ever heard in the late 1940s. Men had been prisoners of war, commandos, aircrew, sailors, Bevin Boys, boffins, captains, privates, in far corners of the earth, on small Scottish islands, or deep in rural England: but war experiences and line-shooting were not the common currency of conversation. There was occasional sensitive awareness of those who seemed to have avoided military service or were in the process of doing so.

Some ex-servicemen were returning to take second degrees, some to complete courses, some to change course, and some to begin at the beginning. I think it was then that for the first time I was aware of the concept of relevance in education; at that time, too, the IQ test was king. After all, the IQ test had almost won us the war: it had, with apparent success, sorted out all manner of people into war jobs they had never dreamt of—it fitted well into the drilled, controlled orderliness of war and of the impending welfare state. We talked with reverence of some who had been shown to have high IQs in tests made available in the psychology department, where Professor Rex Knight held students spell-bound. I did not take psychology myself, mainly to avoid a subject in which my brainy elder brother Roderick had excelled. I seem to remember that attendance at lectures was thin for a day or two once a year, when some of those who were in psychology, or were going in for teaching, were out in the schools giving IQ tests in the great process of separating 11- and 12-year old sheep from goats.

If I had had sensible foresight—or concern for career relevance—I might have extended my service knowledge of wireless and radar to profit from the coming growth of television. For me the choice of English language and literature was a mixture of genuine preference and pleasure, of drift and of soft option—to avoid the mathematics or science required for the Ordinary degree. Certainly a broad based nine-subject Ordinary degree would have been far more relevant than English literature and language as preparation for nearly 30 years in journalism or for my present work in publishing. Some appreciation of politics would have helped, too. I recall little political activity or argument in the university, or indeed in Aberdeen. I can remember two students who were ardent Communists, two Liberals—one histrionic, one ebullient—and one rather suave Conservative. No wonder the Debater was half dead. Compared with, say, Glasgow students—and Glasgow and Aberdeen Universities seem in retrospect to have had many features and qualities in common—Aberdeen probably rated as politically naive or unstretched. Scottish Nationalism was growing then in Glasgow. I recall little nationalist feeling in Aberdeen. Certainly in our studies we had access to little Scottish literature and even less Scottish history. But we were in some measure aware of politics—of the fact that the new principal was strongly Labour, as were Professor Dugald Baird and his wife. There was the new National Health Service (a hot topic at Cornhill); there was instant nationalisation; there was the Berlin airlift, but not yet an anti-nuclear reaction. We were all drawing breath within a reasonably optimistic but austerely rationed society. Food and clothes were in short supply. There was a shortage of paper and textbooks, but not of alcohol, though whisky—when available—was foul stuff. Some of us had acquired drinking capacities in the services and occasionally found the money (£1 sufficed for one evening) to keep in practice. I belonged to the 20 Club created by Barry Symes, science student and talented Show performer. The club met for a dinner once a term. At the conclusion of one heavy evening we ate all the heads off the daffodils with which the hotel had kindly decorated our table.

But it was a prim world in comparison with 20, 30 or 40 years later. The films at Aberdeen's countless cinemas and the plays at H M Theatre (many provided by the Wilson Barrett Company) provoked no arguments about propriety. Donald Wolfit had given me my first experience of professional Shakespeare on stage. Olivier's wartime film *Henry V* augured a new generation of Shakespeare, and a lot of us trooped to see his *Hamlet* and pass erudite judgement on it.

I have referred to the concept of relevance in education: I do so with— at best—puzzlement, not least in reference to university education. In 40 years so much that was thought basic in my own education—indeed was essential for entry to or passage through university—has been abandoned as irrelevant. I am grateful for much of it and often wonder how much of what has displaced it will meet a similar fate. Relevance is remarkably fluid; not like the 'torch of culture' which—as has been argued—it is the duty of education to pass on from one generation to the next. Looking back on my own university education, however, I cannot persuade myself that the content of any one subject or set of subjects is essential to good education. But the character of the teaching is—and the characters who teach.

In the George Herbert hymn, 'Teach me, my God and King', which we sometimes sang in Chapel, there is the verse:

> A man that looks on glass
> On it may stay his eye
> Or, if he pleaseth, through it pass
> And then the heaven espy.

I count myself richly fortunate to have been enabled to espy the heaven of education at King's College. Not invariably, but sometimes. Some dictated lectures—even to the commas—were usually glass of dense opacity. Sometimes it was sensible and safe to stay at glass level, just to be sure of at least passing the examination, for one had not the courage, as it were, to raise one's eyes. In some cases one held on to the glass, learning in later years how to espy heaven through it. For me, Professor Donald Mackinnon's lectures were in this category. In my final year, with Professor Geoffrey Bickersteth as tutor, I espied an especial heaven. One essay per week was prepared, to be read to him in the front room of his house in Queen's Road. He commented on it and asked questions—sometimes kindly, often searching, as often ruthless and bruising. For, as I remember, three or four weeks it was bruising all the way. Then suddenly the glass cleared. My one regret was that the experience came so late. I feel profoundly sorry for those to whom education has not at some stage given this exhilarating experience—a compound of discipline and discovery and delight, of awe and assurance, of humility and humour, and of so much else.

I suppose that my student experience in Shows, *Gaudie*, rectorial campaigns etcetera enabled me to work youth fairly happily out of my system—a process somewhat confused by four years in the services. Far more important, I thank my university for the measure I was afforded of inspiring intellectual experience, an experience to which surely all students should have access, and to which I am sure they can have access in the study of a wide range of subjects, all this provided they meet minds

of the stature and calibre of Mackinnon, Bickersteth, or others to whom
I know students of my acquaintance were as indebted—men like R V
Jones, Alister Hardie, Rex Knight, Clyde Barber and Dugald Baird.

The day before I was to speak at the seminar on student experience, I
happened to meet a professor at another Scottish university who had been
among my contemporaries at Aberdeen. I asked what he would say in my
place. Rather brusquely he quoted Thucydides at me: 'Men, not walls,
make a city'. And it is men—and women—with great minds who make
a university, and enable some lucky students to espy an enduring heaven.

2. RODDY BEGG (Faculties of Arts and Law, 1959–64)

It is difficult to tell how far what I know of the university of my student days is a true recollection, as opposed to knowledge gained during my subsequent employment with the university since May 1966. Over 25 years later, it is difficult to disentangle the two. And I doubt whether I could be described in any way as a 'typical graduate of the 1960s'.

Colin McLaren's comments on the Aberdonian and his university struck a chord. Proceeding from Aberdeen Grammar School to Aberdeen University had been fairly automatic. It was 'just expected', 'unusual to consider going anywhere else'. Indeed, only two of the Aberdeen Grammar sixth form of 1959 went to universities other than Aberdeen—one to Dundee to study dentistry and one to Edinburgh to study engineering (a true individualist!).

In retrospect, the living arrangements of students in the 1950s and 1960s differed in a single but very significant respect from those of the succeeding generations. Until 1960 there were no halls of residence, and students lived at home, in 'digs' or in a flat. Large numbers (including myself) lived at home. One consequence of this was that student life was dominated by the Students' Union on Broad Street, which was the unquestionable social centre of the university. I recall spending many, many hours in the Union: during the daytime on the way between home and classes at King's College; in the late afternoon 'resting' before returning home for tea; and in the evening for society meetings and rehearsals for plays. I have particularly fond memories of the Union's unique catering facilities, when the main course progressed through braised steak on Monday, to stovies on Tuesday, to a remarkable dish called 'American hash' later in the week (no waste in those days!). Linked with memories of the Union are memories of the Dive (now a storeroom) and Wednesday night sessions with 'Sandy West and his Jazzmen'.

Memories that remain include characters on the staff and fellow students, such as Professor Donald Mackinnon (larger in life than in legend), Professor (now Sheriff) Ronnie Ireland and tutorials in his house in Don Street, and the then President of the Socialist Society, Sandy Hobbs. Sandy held his society meetings, it was alleged, in one of the booths in the chipshop next to the Union affectionately known as 'Sweaty Betty's'. Equally fond memories remain of the 'hops' in the Mitchell Hall ('dry' of course) and Jim Moir's Dance Band dominated by the Grammar classics master Ronnie McLeod (known then and to subsequent generations of Grammar boys as 'Tarzan'), who smiled down on his former disciples growing up. For one whose university time outside the law faculty was dominated by dramatic activities, a succession of student shows, and the lifelong friendships made there, were also of particularly rosy memory.

Particular events that stand out include the days of the Cuban missiles crisis, when life seemed to stand still and no one thought of going to classes, but remained in the snack bars in huddled groups exchanging snippets of the latest news as events unfolded. A curious foretaste of things to come was the day when the members of the Union voted whether or not the snackbars would sell Outspan oranges. And so many attended the meeting that it had to be adjourned from the Union Hall to the rear quadrangle at Marischal College, with the speeches delivered from the top of the water storage tank. A narrow vote was won by the anti-apartheid faction, as I recall.

Comparing student life in the 1960s with the two more recent decades, a number of factors appear to dominate. One (already referred to) is the advent of the halls of residence. A second is the rapid expansion in numbers from under 2,000 in 1960 to over 5,000 in 1970; it is no longer possible to vote in the SRC or UMC elections and be able to say confidently that you know every candidate personally. Gone are the older students, back from national service, who once gave a wider spectrum to the student community. For the Aberdeen Grammar School boy, Aberdeen is no longer the automatic choice, and even universities outwith Scotland are an option to be considered. The overall increase in size of the university has also brought changes in the nature of instruction. For a law student in the 1960s the lecture was indistinguishable from a tutorial, as students were able—and encouraged—to participate. By the 1970s, class sizes had grown so as to necessitate the invention of the tutorial and the seminar, to retain this opportunity for student-staff interchange.

In summary, these appear to have been happy days, and memory has certainly burnished that image.

3.   DAVID STRACHAN (Faculty of Divinity, 1970–77)

I had an unusually long time at the university during the 1970s: studying for a B D from 1970 to 1974, taking a sabbatical year as SRC president 1974–5, then returning to do a postgraduate diploma in 1975–6. I was Rector's Assessor to Ian Cuthbertson (1976–77).

The seventies were the decade when the expansion of the university anticipated by the Robbins Report did not happen. Academic buildings had gone up to accommodate the expected influx of new students. Halls of residence began to go up in the sixties but the major amount of building happened in the seventies. The traditional pattern of students staying with landladies was breaking down. The lodgings officers had a hard time obtaining flats or rooms. It was assumed that householders with increasing affluence no longer needed the extra income that a lodger would bring.

Crombie and Johnston were built when budgets were high; Dunbar when they were lower; Adam Smith, Fyfe and Wavell at Hillhead when they were lower yet; and Carnegie Court when they were smaller than had been previously imaginable. There was considerable complaint when Carnegie Court was built. The government was expecting some of these halls of residence to be loan-financed and gave 25 per cent grant towards capital cost only. Previously, halls of residence had been financed entirely by the UGC. Hall fees rose; the government removed from grants information its anticipated breakdown of student spending so that the political weapon which students had used to keep hall fees down was no longer available to them. More of their grant was to be spent on hall fees. To cut costs, dining facilities were amalgamated and reduced in the smaller halls. The building of Hillhead provided a new social centre a long way from the Union, some of whose traditional facilities like baths and laundries became less relevant.

In the halls of residence regulations became looser. There were visiting regulations. Students who were not resident, or students of the opposite sex had to be out of parts of the halls of residence at certain times; but these regulations were gradually relaxed. Adam Smith in Hillhead at some times still locked the doors between the male and female ends at midnight after Fyfe and Wavell had discarded these regulations. Attempts to control an excess number of students staying in halls of residence had to be very carefully phrased in order to avoid any implication of moral judgement. Non-residents had to be out between something like midnight and 5 a.m. Identity cards were required to prevent free meals being taken by non-residents.

The building of a shop and a laundrette at Hillhead further exaggerated the feeling that it was a separate student village. There were some students who never saw Aberdeen beyond a No. 20 bus, who would go down to lectures in the morning, work in the library in the afternoon, and then watch television or go to the bar in the evening. The opening of a bar in Hillhead went some way to reducing high jinks with garden gnomes outside the old cottages on the way to the pub at Balgownie.

Wardens and sub-wardens tried to provide contact between students and get to know them by organising parties and so on, but there were a number of students who kept themselves to themselves. It was possible to stay in the same halls of residence and be in the same class as a student and not talk to him or her.

It is difficult to assess or to compare the sexual behaviour of students with that of previous generations. Freshers' weeks always contained advice from the Student Health Service. Contraception was available, as was always widely reported in *Gaudie*. Halls of residence certainly made sexual relationships easier. Alan Robertson, warden of Hillhead, defending the lack of any visiting regulations, said it was quite ridiculous to suggest that students would be prevented from sexual relationships if they were not allowed in other students' rooms from midnight to 8 o'clock when they could be in those rooms from 8 o'clock to midnight. Not many students were open about whether or not their relationships were sexual. But a survey was done in the early 1970s which indicated that a significant number were. One warden, commenting on the uncertainty of what was happening, said 'you didn't know what was going on in the next room, but you wished it was happening to you'.

The university largely missed the turmoil of the sixties. The SRC was not very political although the seventies produced at least two MPs from the SRC, one President of NUS, and one of NUS Scotland. There was one very significant demonstration in 1971 against Mrs Thatcher (then Education Secretary) and her attempts to reform the financing of student unions. In the late seventies the administration building was occupied in protest at the university's investments in multinational companies with South African links.

Reform of the constitution to tilt the balance of power towards general meetings and away from a representative council seemed quite irrelevant to that majority of students who rarely turned up—especially medics and Marischal-based scientists.

In 1974–5 the SRC was lobbying for full membership of Senatus and in 1976 for representation on Court. The SRC resisted pressure for it to amalgamate with the Union or the Athletic Association as had happened in other universities. There was a certain amount of suspicion about co-operation between the three bodies. The Composite Matriculation Fee Dispersement Committee rarely, if ever, required adjudication from the Finance Committee although there were some arguments over special projects, the SRC championing the cause of Campus Radio, with a transmitter supposed to be strung across Crombie towers. This was dropped in favour of the ski slope at Balgownie.

The SRC was a little isolated in King Street. The book agency and the travel service drew students down to its building. When the travel service moved to the Union and the switchboard for the organisations was centralised also at the Union it was time for a move to the King's campus.

A lot of the SRC's work was in welfare: dealing with grants problems, accommodation, representing students with individual problems to the university. The university was concerned that its reputation as a happy university should be preserved as it evolved from a small community to a larger, more diverse one. In the mid seventies a review of welfare provision was carried out.

Gaudie lurched from one style to another as its editors came and went. Cynicism about all institutions was sometimes informed, sometimes not. To attract advertising, and to cut administration, it became a free sheet. It became the magazine of all Aberdeen students, but for most university undergraduates, RGIT might as well have been in Timbuctoo.

Chapter 6

Structures and Processes of Internal Government

JENNIFER CARTER

The structures and processes of internal government changed less than many other aspects of university life in the period 1945 to 1981. The extent and the rate of change were limited, both because the challenges to traditional forms of authority were relatively mild at Aberdeen, and because the constitution of the university was embedded in statute law and so not easily altered. An impulse for change came from the growing size of the university, and this did indeed affect governmental structures and processes, though perhaps not as much as might have been expected in an institution where the undergraduate population quadrupled, and the academic staff were eight times as numerous in 1980–1 as they had been in 1945–6.

At Aberdeen, in common with most British universities, but in sharp contrast to many universities in Europe and America, these were peaceful decades. Outside political pressures and the great protest movements of the 1960s and 1970s made very little impression here, while the internal challenge to traditional staff hierarchies was also muted.[1] Compare our experience of student protest with, for instance, that of a fellow historian at Wisconsin, who writes in a recent memoir:

> In the dead time of night in the summer of 1970, I was jolted out of a deep sleep by a huge explosion. The bombing of the Army Mathematical Research Centre in the heart of the university was the climax, one realised only later, of protests ... against the Vietnam War. ... But before that sad night the protests had increased in intensity and ranged from countless meetings of opposition—not just to the war but to the university as well— to the storming of faculty meetings. ... The Wisconsin National Guard in full combat gear descended upon the campus at one point and remained for two weeks.[2]

We were indeed living in a different world at Aberdeen. The most serious events we faced in the peak years of student protest were one small demonstration and three sit-ins. The demonstration, during which the gates of Marischal College were chained shut as an expression of solidarity with the students at the London School of Economics, ended quickly when the buildings officer told the students concerned that fire regulations required the gates to be open. The first sit-in (admittedly it was said to be the first such happening in a Scottish university) was in the Registry, and concerned failure rates. The second, again at the Registry, was a spin-off from a more serious protest at Edinburgh about files kept on individual students. Each of these events lasted only a few hours. The third, and more serious, sit-in was a two-week occupation of the whole University Office at Regent Walk. This was in protest against the university's holding shares in companies operating in South Africa. At the time many attributed the occupation to a mixture of youthful idealism and the impatient ambition of the then president of the SRC. If the latter part of the explanation has any truth, that president was untypical. Most student representatives were characterised by a high degree of reasonableness and responsibility. They were easily recognisable as 'students who are prepared to sit on committees and reach consensus', and 'worthy rather than newsworthy'.[3] Equally, it must be recorded that potential student opposition was managed with great political skill by Principal Wright. Wright was perceived by many students as someone who was genuinely on their side, and interested in individual student careers and general student welfare. A key institutional change was the creation in December 1968 of the University Committee. At this committee the principal and six senior members of Court and Senatus met regularly and informally with seven representatives of the SRC 'to review matters of mutual interest'. This committee continued its valuable behind-the-scenes work until student representatives became direct participants in university government.

Aberdeen was long accustomed to some student participation in its internal government, through the student-elected office of rector. R D Anderson shows clearly how influential the student voice was even in the nineteenth century, both through the rectorship and through the newly created SRC.[4] In our period students moved from indirect to direct participation in university government, joining the governing institutions at all levels from departmental consultative committees, through faculties and Senatus, to the Court. The process of direct participation began in a natural way when Jo Grimond, rector in 1970, nominated as his assessor on Court a newly-graduated student who had just completed his term of office as secretary of the SRC. From 1979 rectors began to nominate as their assessors the serving presidents of the SRC, who were usually undergraduate students, and in the 1980s the president was co-opted to membership. No serious problem seems to have arisen from student participation in the different levels of university government, although it caused many staff much anxiety at the time it began.

When the Committee on Internal Academic Government (the Meston Committee) sat from 1973 to 1977 the issue of student membership of Senatus was a major concern. The committee finally recommended the abolition of the then existing Senatus Staff-Student Consultative Committee, in favour of students being directly represented on Senatus. Lengthy debates preceded this conclusion, which was only reached over the recorded dissent of two members of the committee. While from the later 1980s the Meston Report looks like a very cautious document, one area in which it did bring about significant change was in forwarding direct student participation in internal government. The challenge—if that is not to give it too strong a title—from the student body was thus a fairly mild one, which gained within a decade its immediate object of direct student participation in university government. Similarly, the challenge from staff to the traditional governing structures was smoothly accommodated, though direct participation by non-professorial staff beyond the level of faculty required legislative change.

If one reason for the relatively slow changes in the institutions and processes of internal government was that challenges presented to the existing order were mild, a second and perhaps more important reason was that Aberdeen was governed under act of parliament, and its constitution therefore required considerable effort to alter. Acts of parliament dating back to 1858 provided the constitutional framework for all the older Scottish universities. Any significant change had to be agreed by all four universities and carried through parliament by the Scottish Office. The only major change in the period 1945 to 1981 was made by the Universities (Scotland) Act of 1966. The main point of this act was to give direct representation in the internal government of the university, beyond the level of faculty, to non-professorial staff. At Aberdeen the act provided that the number of Senatus assessors on the Court be increased from four to six 'of whom at least two shall be readers or lecturers'. At the same time, 'the Senatus Academicus of each of the older Universities shall include a number of readers and lecturers of that University equal to not less than one-third of the number of persons who are members of that Senatus'.

The memories of those most involved suggest that the main demand for the 1966 changes came from outside Aberdeen, mainly from AUT (Scotland). Perhaps Aberdeen's contribution had come at an earlier stage, as is suggested by the historian of the General Council, referring to episodes in 1913 and 1946.[5] During the period 1945 to 1966 a few non-professorial staff were regularly co-opted to membership of Senatus, and others attended by special invitation, for instance when they were acting as heads of department. On the eve of the 1966 changes, the non-professorial delegation which met the UGC during their 1965 visitation recorded that:

> this university is more liberal in respect of non-professorial representation on the Senatus Academicus ... than are some other universities.

Can we trace any specific effect of non-professorial participation in Senatus and Court when membership by right and election, and on a larger scale, replaced the small-scale and occasional representation of non-professorial staff before 1966? It does not seem that qualitatively the changes were dramatic, though quantitatively they did make a difference. Non-professors elected to Senatus and Court, like the students who followed them onto those bodies, were highly responsible individuals, not in the business of rocking the boat. (With hindsight, perhaps some gentle boat-rocking might have been a valuable contribution to the affairs of the university?) But there was a big change in the size of the university's two main governing bodies, as a result of the 1966 act taken together with the expansion of staff numbers. Senatus had already almost doubled in size between 1945 and 1965, and now it was set to grow further, more than doubling again before 1980. The Court too began to grow, though more gently, after 1966.

In addition to these changes in size, there was some change of atmosphere after 1966, which had to do with the age-structure of the academic community. With a retiring age set until 1967 at the age of 70 for non-clinical academics, and with an informal seniority rule prevailing for much longer in such matters as the appointment of deans and the election of Senatus assessors to the Court, the university did tend to be run by oldish men, and by people who had served very long terms in office. When the author joined the Court as one of its first two non-professorial Senatus assessors in 1967, aged 34, the average age of the other members of Court was 62, and some of them had been serving on Court for twenty years. Non-professorial assessors, and doubtless the students who followed them onto the Court, sometimes felt that they were representing a different university from the one with which many seniors were familiar. The non-professorial assessors were treated with great courtesy by Principal Wright, and went without question onto the two main committees—the Finance Committee and the Edilis and Lands Committee—which in those days were simply the Court meeting under a different name. Non-professorial assessors were easily socialised by the Court. On Senatus it was even harder for non-professorial staff to make a distinctive contribution, partly because that body was already so large. Thus the tangible effects on university government of including non-professorial academics in the main decision-making bodies of the university were small. Their inclusion did, however, recognise the swing in the balance of staff from professors and assistants (the prevailing pattern in the 1940s) to professors and lecturers (the prevailing pattern from the 1950s onwards). The arrival of non-professorial representatives on Senatus was immediately preceded by the creation of the Committee of Principal, Vice-Principal and Deans. This new body was empowered to deal with any matter referred to it by Senatus, especially in the sphere of discipline. Some saw the committee as intended to be a safeguard against an enlarged Senatus, but it was never in practice used in that way. What it was, perhaps, was a signal that Senatus was already too big a body to continue conducting all its business in traditional ways.

While the growth in the size of Senatus is obvious, the growing size of the Court is significant too. Nominal membership does not tell the whole story, and Table 1 shows at five-yearly intervals the number of meetings held and the average attendance at them. (For this purpose the purely formal meetings of Senatus which used to be held to authenticate graduations are ignored.) Several interesting observations may be drawn from this pattern of meetings. Average attendance at Court was always high (and non-attenders were often people with the least direct involvement in the university, such as the City representatives, or rectors who were absentees) whereas at Senatus the gap between attendance and membership was widening after 1966. The Senatus absentees increased in number, though on the figures in Table 1 not as a proportion of total membership, except in 1975–6 when average attendance was less than half of the total membership. Taking attendances together with the incidence of meetings, we might deduce that the two main governing bodies of the university were becoming more formalised after the mid-1960s. At the beginning of the period Court and Senatus were each meeting monthly, except for the summer vacations, and Senatus was attended by only twice the number of people at Court, remaining quite an intimate debating body. By the end of the period meetings of both bodies were less frequent (though for Court it must be remembered that most members were still meeting twice in between Court meetings as members of the Finance and Edilis Committees), while Senatus suffered the double disadvantage of being too large an assembly for effective discussion, and one with a significant number of backwoodsmen.

Part at least of this problem was keenly appreciated in the 1970s, and the Meston Committee spent a lot of its time debating the size, composition and effectiveness of the Senatus. In the end it came down in favour of changes only of detail, for instance, the exclusion of professors who were not heads of department, and the introduction of Principal's Question Time. It rejected both the idea of a smaller, fully elected Senatus, and the idea of a strong Senatus steering committee. Indeed, it looked somewhat

TABLE 1   MEETINGS OF COURT AND SENATUS, 1945–81

| | COURT | | SENATUS | |
	Meetings	Average attendance	Meetings	Average attendance
1945–46	15	10	10	20
1950–51	13	9	11	31
1955–56	13	9	10	30
1960–61	14	11	10	30
1965–66	12	10	13	42
1970–71	10	14	8	59
1975–76	9	15	10	59
1980–81	9	18	8	93

suspiciously at the existing Committee of Principal, Vice-Principal and Deans:

> Suggestions were received that the Committee might act as a business or steering committee for the Senatus. This has not been part of its role in the past and it is felt that it is not really desirable to give it more authority than it already possesses. ... Care should be exercised in selecting the type of business to be referred to the Committee.

Evidence was taken at the Meston Committee about the Educational Policy Committee at Edinburgh University, but no recommendation emerged to give Aberdeen a nudge towards more directive planning. In fairness to the Meston Committee it must be recorded that its brief was to look only at the academic government of the university, and that if still in the late 1980s there are powerful academic voices discounting the need for, or even the possibility of centralised university planning, there were far more such voices in the 1970s.

Yet the gap, as it now appears, in the governmental structures and processes of the 1960s and 1970s was the failure to create adequate mechanisms for planning. If, as was argued above, Court and Senatus were becoming more formalised, it may now be suggested that this did not result in business going elsewhere (as conspiracy theory might suggest) but in the neglect of an important function, namely planning. John Hargreaves, in Chapter 1, has shown how the small-scale university of the 1940s and 1950s could plan quite effectively, but how in the 1960s and 1970s planning became more incoherent, as well as being inevitably more subject to outside influences, especially from the UGC. The academic community agonised over whether to expand the university, and if so by how much, but it never seems to have debated what sort of university

Aberdeen should try to become: it was rather a question of 'stay as we are' versus 'more of the same'. Thus academic objectives were prioritised by faculties and Senatus, and costed by Court, but there were only fitful attempts to link Court and Senatus in a central planning process. From 1968 onwards there was a University Planning Committee, replacing the joint Court-Senatus Estimates Committees which had previously prepared quinquennial estimates and memoranda for UGC visitations. But this Planning Committee does not seem to have taken any more positive and continuous a role than the quinquennial committees had done. On the eve of the crisis of 1981 a review of university committee structures produced a new joint Court-Senatus Planning Committee, which bore the brunt of that crisis for the next two years. It is difficult to avoid the conclusion that Aberdeen suffered from its failure to plan effectively. To many academics from the 1940s to the 1980s the university seemed over-centralised, with virtually all governmental power concentrated in the Court, controlling as it did finance, external relations and appointments. Yet paradoxically the Court waited, with constitutional propriety, for the Senatus to tell it what shape the university ought to take. Senatus, especially in the 1960s and 1970s, lacked full knowledge of financial matters and external circumstances, as well as being too incoherent a body itself to contribute effectively to the planning process. It was not until the early stages of the crisis of 1981 that Senatus began to demand more financial information than could be gleaned from annual accounts and estimates.

The need for a linkage between Court and Senatus on planning was hidden at the time because the two bodies co-existed with apparently little friction. To take one small but not untypical example of the sort of harmony that prevailed, we might notice the retiral of that long-serving and masterful Secretary, Colonel Butchart. On 28 February 1951 the principal told Senatus that Colonel Butchart would retire at the end of the next session, and:

> stated that the Court would wish to know the views, if any, of the Senatus on any changes in the general frame of University Administration which they considered desirable.

Senatus promptly appointed a committee, chaired by the principal, to consider this matter. It came back to the next Senatus meeting with sensible observations—including 'that the man appointed should not exceed 50 years of age'—and these observations were passed on to the Court. In contrast, one of the very few instances of open disharmony which is obvious from the formal record arose in 1961. Some senators were worried about the financial conservatism, as they saw it, of the Court, and they secured a debate on the propositions that more money should be unlocked from reserves, and a national appeal for donations be launched. At the same time there was pressure in Senatus for additional academic staff, and for more promotions. The Court fended off these criticisms by referring them to the Quinquennial Estimates Committee, and no appeal for funds was launched. Senators were still feeling sore when the memoranda submitted to the UGC were revealed to Senatus a little later. Professor Allen of engineering commented that he would have appreciated it if the whole Senatus could have seen the memorandum about the teaching of engineering before it was sent up to the UGC.

The circulation of information at all levels, or internal communication, and with it the involvement of staff in the government of the university, was increasingly seen as a problem after the mid 1950s. The non-professorial committee which met the UGC in 1965 deplored the apathy of non-professorial staff towards the affairs of the university, saying:

> Our enquiries suggest that this apathy stems very largely from the fact that many of the staff have no responsibility for the conduct of their departmental affairs, still less for those of the university.

Perhaps in response to the well-argued non-professorial document, the UGC in its visitorial report gently hinted that:

> The University might care to consider whether any regular arrangements for consulting the academic staff could be adopted.

Again, in their 1969 report, the UGC:

> Noted the desire of the non-professorial staff to contribute to the policy making of the University. ... some apprehension had been voiced over communication throughout the University.

Presumably before the mid 1950s, with fewer than 300 full-time academic staff, news circulated naturally around the community—or perhaps too few staff wanted to know what was going on for internal communication to be a big issue? By the mid 1960s the issue was on the agenda and in the 1970s the Meston Committee shows that there was considerable uncertainty about how best to discharge what was by then seen as a responsibility to circulate information within the university, and indeed to tell the outside world a little about what we were doing. The Meston Committee recommended that members of staff should have access, through departments and libraries, to the approved non-confidential minutes of Senatus and Court. The idea of appointing a university information officer was explicitly rejected.

Faculties and boards of studies widened their membership greatly between the 1940s and 1970s. Science faculty adopted a faculty board system, with the proviso that this steering committee could be over-ruled by a full faculty meeting—normally faculty boards attracted a bigger attendance than faculty itself. Arts and social sciences eventually opted for an open faculty—and there attendance fell to new lows. Nevertheless, faculties and boards of studies in this period handled a large volume of business. For instance, medical faculty carried through the redesign of the medical curriculum, while in arts and sciences the faculties accomplished considerable changes in the balance of the degree system, from the traditional Ordinary to the mainly Honours degree, and from the old-style Ordinary MA to a much more permissive modern version.

At departmental level little changed formally, but it is here that we should be particularly aware of changes of process rather than structure. In the 1940s there can have been little collegiality between professors and other staff. Only professors enjoyed tenure: lecturers had their contracts annually renewed, and assistants were seldom kept beyond the customary three years of their appointments. The university was manned mainly by professors and assistants. Lecturers and assistants often did not have even the basic amenity of a room to work in. A distinguished academic who began his career here in the postwar period recalls that so little was provided for poorly paid assistants like himself that they begged examination stationery from the sacrist to write their lectures on. By the 1970s much of this had changed, though it is difficult to date the process. In 1975 a symbol of changed conditions may be seen in the fact that at the UGC visitation the non-professorial staff were, for the first time, not separately represented. Five years earlier the first exchange of the headship of a department between two professors had taken place, and in 1977 there was even to be the appointment of a non-professorial head of a department which included two professors.

Another area of change was in the relationship of departments and their heads with the central administration of the university. At the beginning of our period professors who were heads of department were in a very powerful, what is often termed a baronial, position. Their own tenure was secure, they had a major influence in appointing lecturing staff, and their assistants were simply nominated at their own discretion. In subjects where there was no great demand on university resources for support staff and equipment, the professorial head of a department was the monarch of all he surveyed. In contrast, by the end of our period, departments were much more answerable to central control. Support staff and equipment were needed, at least to some extent, by every department, and these were now expensive commodities rationed by central committees. Assistants had long gone, and lecturing staff had gained their own status in the university, for instance through membership of its senior governing bodies. Most departments had instituted departmental meetings and all were encouraged to do so. There was much less freedom of action for the professor or departmental head. The contrast between the 1940s and 1970s is clear, but the stages by which things changed from one state to the other is not, and no doubt experience differed a good deal from one department to another.

On the non-academic side of university life, welfare services were able to make their voices heard, especially the student health service. A 1950 report from the redoubtable Dr Macklin 'regarding the lack of outside interests among students', led to a motion being proposed—but not formally put to the vote in Senatus—'that all medically fit students whose National Service had been deferred and who were not conscientious objectors should be required to join the University Air Squadron or the Training Corps for two years'. Another kind of welfare agency, the advisers of studies in arts, were given some status by being admitted to membership of faculty before this became open to all. When halls of residence came on the scene their wardens were not so easily fitted into the traditional governing structures, but at least from 1969 the convener of the committee of wardens and senior residents had a seat on Senatus, and from 1976 an Academic and Welfare Services Committee began to operate.

Trades unions made slow headway at Aberdeen. The AAUT was founded in 1921, but before the Second World War its role seems to have been mainly social. During the war it fought a brisk engagement with the Court to secure recognition as the official negotiating body responsible for fire watching duties carried out by members of staff. In the later 1940s and the 1950s it helped to promote useful reforms, including the creation of the university careers service, and it generated a lively atmosphere of debate in the Inter-Faculty Group.[6] Gradually it moved more into the role of a trades union, and was officially recognised in 1971. Other staff unions, ASTMS, AUEW, GMW and NUPE, were similarly recognised in 1970; the TGWU in 1972; and NALGO in 1974. Although the 'campus unions' (including the AAUT and the SRC) occasionally campaigned together, it could not be said that they had a large impact on university government.

The precise role of the University Office remains rather mysterious to outsiders: not sinister, but difficult to evaluate. Whether the Office was merely the servant of its academic masters, and of its head, the principal, or whether it had scope to innovate in policy matters is not easy to establish. (Tom Skinner's comments in the appendix are especially welcome as an insider's view of the Office.) Clearly successive Secretaries of the university played a major part in its affairs. In Colonel Butchart's day it was popularly held that he, together with Dr Ross (a long-serving and powerful member of Court) really ran everything between them. A nice example of their style in action concerns the Chemistry Building, which, when it was already under construction, had an extra floor added at the behest of Butchart and Ross, without reference even to our UGC paymasters. Earlier tribute has been paid to Mr W S Angus, who in his time as Secretary did so much to prepare the way for expansion.

The other senior officers of the university kept their ancient places without major alteration in our period. Thus, the chancellor did those things chancellors do; and the chancellor's assessor was always among the most active members of Court. The rectors of this period varied in their assiduity. With the exception of Grimond, they probably made comparatively little impact on the government of the institution. The rector who made the highest claims at the time of his appointment disappointed most in the performance of his duties. Mr Frank Thomson, at his election in 1966, not only said that he would be a real working rector, but also (according to *Gaudie*) claimed:

> I regard this as a victory for the ordinary man ... The bonfires are burning ... for a man who came from the heather and broke through the mists enshrouding the Establishment.[7]

No doubt 'the Establishment' was mildly relieved when, shortly afterwards, Mr Thomson departed for America.

The principal, as head of 'the Establishment' had an increasingly hard job in this period, not only with a mounting work load within the university, but with ever increasing demands for external contacts, especially with the UGC and CVCP. Each of those who held office in this period brought individual talents and distinction to the job, and it remained true throughout the period that the principal was the single most important person in the university. He bridged crucial areas—internal-external affairs, Court-Senatus relations, and the connection of academics with administrators. In February 1961 the ill-health of Principal Taylor led to the appointment of the first vice-principal in the modern history of the university, Professor Edward Maitland Wright, who was later to be Taylor's successor and to hold office through all the problems of the expansion period. The formal suggestion that a vice-principal be appointed came from Senatus, and a joint Court-Senatus Committee worked out the specifications of the job. In a list of 69 committees, most chaired by the principal, the vice-principal was to take over as chairman of ten, but more significantly he was to 'be prepared to act as the Principal's deputy in matters retained by the Principal'. Oral evidence suggests that there was much more to the job than appeared on the surface. One thing that the vice-principal does not seem to have done at first, although he did do this later, was to share with the principal the burden of chairing appointment committees. Given the huge expansion of staff during the 1960s and 1970s this must indeed have been a time-consuming job, as well as being one which so deeply affected the future of the university. Back in the 1940s and into the 1950s, the Court itself was still active in making appointments, rather than simply ratifying the choices of its committees. At some point custom changed, and by the later 1960s it was well established practice for the Court simply to accept the recommendations of appointing committees.

An extraordinary case in 1946 stood out in the minutes, which may serve to introduce one last theme. An appointing committee short-listing for a senior post in the Library queried whether it might bring forward a woman candidate. The Court confirmed that a woman would be eligible for the job. The committee then brought two names to the Court, one of a man and the other of a woman candidate. At the last moment the man withdrew his application and the woman alone was interviewed. The Court then decided to make no appointment until a male candidate was forthcoming, and when one was, he was appointed. This is but one curious incident which may have many possible explanations. Certainly it does not suggest that the Court or its appointing committees, even in the 1940s, was necessarily biased against women candidates for jobs.[8] And yet Table III in the Statistical Appendix, showing staff numbers, must raise disquieting questions. Is it not remarkable that in the whole history of the university to date we have appointed only two women professors? Is it not striking that during the expansion of staff numbers around the 1960s the proportion of women among the full-time academic staff actually fell? The highest proportion of women on the full-time academic staff was 16 per cent in 1945–6—almost double the 8.8 per cent in the same category of staff in 1980–1. The high proportions of women staff at the end of the war may have owed something to wartime conditions, but it did not owe everything to them: only five professors, ten lecturers and sixteen assistants were away on war service. It is not easy to judge how unusual Aberdeen was in its proportions of women staff. The authoritative study of British academics, published in 1971, accords women only the briefest mention, saying that:

> they still constitute a small minority of 10 per cent who tend to concentrate in the lower ranks and in the faculties of arts and social studies.[9]

On the other hand, UGC statistics show that by 1980 the proportion of women academic staff in all British universities had grown to 13.9 per cent.[10] This may suggest that Aberdeen was becoming increasingly untypical.

Universities are such complex and idiosyncratic institutions that it is difficult to get strictly comparable data about them. As in the simple case of women staff numbers, so also it is not possible to judge how unusual we were in the much more complex area of internal government. If, as many critics hold, the processes were slow and the structures over-centralised at Aberdeen, is this peculiar to Aberdeen, or is it a comment more generally applicable to university government in Britain? The structures and processes of internal government here may be viewed as rather hidebound, traditionalist and unable to meet the growing imperative of university-level planning. Alternatively they may be seen as traditional but flexible, coping reasonably well with very great changes in the life of the university. Whichever interpretation is preferred, it seems clear that between 1945 and 1981 changes in internal government came more slowly than in other areas of university life.

Commentary to Chapter 6

University Government: a Comment

T B SKINNER

Dr Carter suggests that the structure and processes of internal government changed less than might have been expected. This may be true; but I invite you to add to Dr Carter's suggested reasons for this, the idea that the main structure at least survived because it was fitted to its purpose, whatever the change in size or emphasis of the university. The structure and indeed the internal government exist only to further the academic ends of the university, government and administration having no justification whatever as ends in themselves. A supreme academic body consisting of academics is therefore surely right; it was clearly robust enough to absorb a leavening of what was, I suppose, consumer representation and of a welfare voice without disruption. And it was essential that academics should be the largest single group, with enormous influence beyond its own numbers, on the Court, the body charged with managing and distributing resources and employing staff.

The beauty of the nineteenth-century Scottish University Acts is that, while they were enacted, at least in my view, chiefly to bridle the anarchic academics whose antics were uncovered by the Royal Commissions—and what a choice field for historic research all that material is—this was done with a delicacy that retained the superiority of the academics and recognised that academic institutions are neither ivory towers nor grocers' shops. The two-headed beast worked. Long before our period began in 1945, the quirky statutory provision of an appeal to the Court against any decision of the Senatus had ceased to matter, and the central structure was sound. So that when Dr Carter, with the air of one regretting that she cannot announce the fall of the Bastille, impishly suggests that it might have been a good idea if the newly enfranchised junior staff and students had rocked the boat a bit, I believe she means no more than that. In the midst of a colossal national and local expansion that was surely at least morally well-motivated, but which would have torn an unsound structure to shreds, the 1966 Act merely enhanced, fairly superficially, what was already in place. I do not believe there was much for the older universities to learn or adopt from the later experiments in structure of the new foundations, though one must admire the courageous and not unsuccessful work done in trying new patterns, notably in Scotland by Tom Cottrell at Stirling.

Dr Carter went on to suggest that the university ducked the issue of effective central planning in the 1960s and 1970s; and that the processes of internal government here, perhaps in common with all UK universities, were rather slow and rather over-centralised. Of central planning, from where I was sitting during the last thirteen years of our period, I could see none worth a straw, but for good reasons. One reason, which was also responsible for the rather slow processes in decision making, was not over-centralisation, but on the contrary an admirable though perhaps clumsy willingness or even determination, as our period progressed, to secure the approval of those actually doing the job at the coalface. I bet it did not feel like that at the coalface, and it was probably only in the late 1960s that respect for the autonomy of heads of departments began to be replaced by respect for consensus within each department.

Be that as it may, I do not think my memory is false in recalling the great Sir Edward Wright, who was a pragmatist more at home in the Court than in the Senate, saying in effect 'Oh dear!—does this mean it (whatever 'it' was) has to go all the way down the ladder and up again?' But of course he knew this was right. It was right that the material on which the Court made resource-allocation decisions came from depart- ments, came from faculties, came from committees on which academics predominated. But it did not lead to quick decisions, and, whatever it felt like, it lacked the prompt incisiveness possible with centralisation or with dictatorship. Proper consultation is not, however, incompatible with firm government, once you have determined who is to exercise it, or indeed by itself incompatible with strategic planning. Dr Carter spoke rather disparagingly of the Quinquennial Estimates. I personally thought the visitations of the full UGC were a farce, though very enjoyable; but the preparation of the estimates was a real opportunity and a useful exercise for those who cared about the university as a whole, always fewer than one could wish; certainly when inflation and fear of an apparently open-ended financial commitment led to abandonment nationally of the aim— never actually achieved—of five-year rolling planning, it was hopeless to pretend to be doing much more than considering individual problems and proposals in series.

Perhaps even so my recollection of no effective long-term or even medium-term planning will seem in time to be, or perhaps actually will be, at variance with the historical record. Even Cabinet memos and minutes, read from day to day as they actually record discussion and decision (instant history, as it were), give the impression of little time being devoted to big issues of policy compared with the amount of attention necessarily given to immediate problems, and perhaps I was too close. There were few attempts at major strategic change. The best example I can recall was George Burnett's attempt to unpick the rather untidy tangle of engineering relations with RGIT by in effect absorbing the engineering wing of both institutions into a single school or faculty. Our Senatus rejected the proposals, and clearly the political will was absent from both bodies—one of the might-have-beens, like an English victory at Bannockburn, whose contemplation is, I believe, discouraged by real historians; but weighing the pros and cons at this distance, in the light of subsequent and continuing events, may not be an entirely unfruitful pastime. But even this example, which I have called an attempt at major strategic change (whether the decision was negative or positive is irrelevant in this connection), is not an example of planning but essentially only an attempt to solve one problem. We must remember, as Dr Carter hinted, that this university was, until about halfway through our period, for over 450 years, shockingly poor. Of course, Aberdonians are far from mean; but those who have passed through this university and gone on to make a fortune—there must surely have been more than a handful—have not, with a few honourable exceptions, felt the urge to remember their blessed mother other than sentimentally. When the universities began to be used nationally as an economic springboard in the sixties, government money was given to this university to spend, not to stash away against lean years. At an earlier seminar we have spoken about the pressure to commit the university to further expansion even after the period for which government funding was committed shrank to effectively less than twelve months. My hindsight is not acute enough to spot a point at which, by planning to pursue different academic goals and change the emphasis, scope, and shape of the university, the Senatus and Court could have prolonged the fatter years.

I am surprised that Dr Carter should find 'the precise role of the University Office ... very mysterious': a comment difficult to comprehend from somebody who has served on Court and Senatus and played an academic and a welfare role second to none. I get some help to understanding, however, in her reference to the office as 'the central administration of the university'. Whatever the situation in the first half of the century, when Colonel Butchart, virtually alone in the office, stamped his personality on a much smaller institution in a manner that would not be acceptable nowadays, for most of our period it has not been accurate to regard the office as synonymous or coterminous with the central administration. This is the misunderstanding that leads to the nonsense of occupying the University Office to express dissatisfaction with 'the administration'—with decisions certainly not taken by office staff—so incidentally disrupting services to students and everyone else. The office is simply a group of university servants implementing decisions properly taken by others and trying to make sure that it all works. Individual officers may be invited to contribute to discussion, not by right but because their experience is relevant; but the chief contribution of the office to major decisions is servicing the bodies involved. Its duty is the same to all members of the university, to students and staff alike, something a few academics seem to find scarcely credible. The growth in the office during our period was simply in response to increased demand for its services; incidentally if one can trust UGC statistics in this matter, Aberdeen was in 1981, as I am told it was in the 1940s, one of the three universities in Britain devoting the lowest proportion of its expenditure to 'administration', a UGC heading chiefly made up of office salaries. The office runs some necessary formal services (e.g., Registry); it manages within Court policy a large if shrinking estate through the deliciously named Edilis; it runs some welfare services (e.g., Careers); it is an agency, a pair of hands, for the university as employer (e.g., calculating and paying wages)—and so on. I thought everyone would have noticed all this, despite the lower profile its officers have been taught to adopt. So where's the mystery? The office may rightly regard itself as essential if the show is to go on, but, just as clearly as university government more generally, the office must be treated as a means not an end, helping to create a community in which academic ends can be achieved.

Chapter 7

The University and the State

I G C HUTCHISON

Before 1945, the University Grants Committee had a much less significant impact on Aberdeen University than it was to acquire. The committee had been formed in 1919 to advise the government on the financial needs of universities and the extent to which state finance should be given to meet these needs. In common with most other universities, Aberdeen derived most of its income from other sources, particularly fees and endowments. Finance for capital projects was frequently provided by individual benefactors (notably for founding chairs), by the Carnegie Trust and other interested bodies. The medical complex at Foresterhill, the university's major building project of the inter-war era, is a prime example of multi-sourced funding. In the inter-war years, however, the central aspects of the UGC's role and *modus operandi* as they were to be applied for most of the period under review were well established. The latter included: the visitation every five years; the quinquennial allocation; the allocation of a block grant, with only very general advice as to its distribution; the submission of statements of requirements by the universities. As to the former, the UGC was seen as a buffer mediating between the university system and the government, advising the latter as to the financial needs of the universities, but determining without state interference the distribution of the global sum awarded. So the independence of the universities was protected, but the government was given the most accurate possible assessment of the financial position of universities.

After the Second World War, universities became increasingly dependent on the committee for the bulk of their finance for capital and recurrent expenditure—Aberdeen was no exception. The most significant factor was the marked expansion of universities after the war, a process over and above the immediate post-1945 influx of war veterans. A series of committees reported to the government between 1944 and 1948 on a range of subject areas—some of the most important being: science and technology (the Barlow Committee); social science (the Clapham Committee); the demand for school teachers; agriculture (the Alness Committee); medical education (the Goodenough Committee). All of them called for a sizeable growth in the provision of university places in the relevant subject, and the government endorsed the conclusions, putting extra money in the way of the UGC to let universities meet these commitments. Aberdeen benefited from this growth phase, for instance in medicine, agriculture and social science, as new staff were appointed and departments moved into new fields of teaching and research. In consequence recurrent grant rose from £53,000 in 1944–5 to £130,000 in 1947–8.

But as a result of the increased state funding and of the perceived greater centrality of universities to the economic and social development of the country which this flow of reports engendered, the government redefined the purpose of the UGC. Whereas hitherto its remit had been to advise the government on the needs of the universities, now it was to advise the state on how universities could meet 'national needs' and it was to encourage universities to respond to these needs. In the prevailing post-war mood of consensus, the CVCP endorsed this shift of emphasis by pledging the willingness of universities to co-operate. A direct implication of the new scope of the UGC was pointed out by Sir John Anderson, the Chancellor of the Exchequer, to a delegation of members of universities' courts— including Colonel Birnie Reid, the Aberdeen representative. Anderson was reported as stating 'that it might be advisable for the Universities to seek suggestions and guidance from the Universities Grants Committee to an extent greater than has been done in the past'.[1]

Despite warnings like that, the period between 1945 and the implementation of the Robbins Committee Report has been seen by commentators as one of relatively loose UGC supervision, in contrast to the subsequent eras of ever tighter central co-ordination. Yet in some respects Aberdeen soon experienced greater direct involvement in its affairs by the Committee, as it took a close and critical look at various projects. Sometimes it took a positive lead: in 1947 it encouraged an increase in postgraduate scholarships; in the same year it suggested the establishment of research staff in fats, oils, detergents; and in 1948 pushed for the extension of staffing in plant physiology and ecology beyond the botany professor's original request. On the other hand, it deployed its influence to express disapproval: in 1947 it withheld some earmarked funding until clinical medical teaching was reorganised in conformity with the Goodenough Report; in 1952 it rejected an application to establish an engineering department under

Professor Allan quite independent of Robert Gordon's Institute; in 1948 it cut back the planned growth of agriculture to what it saw as more realistic levels. The quality of furnishings proposed for Crombie Hall was pored over in detail lest they be too luxurious, and careful costing of all building projects was demanded before approval was given.

The acceptance by the government in 1963 of the Robbins Report is customarily seen as the start of the major expansion in universities, but under Sir Keith Murray's chairmanship, the UGC had from the late 1950s initiated a growth programme of substantial dimensions. The university was invited in 1960 to raise its student population from around 2,500 to 4,500 within a decade, and sanction was given for the construction of the Natural Philosophy and new Arts (Taylor) Buildings as well as further halls of residence on a scale to cope. These developments were controlled by the UGC largely through its building programme. Aberdeen had learned from the problems of erecting the Chemistry Building that UGC funding was indispensable. Colonel Butchart and Dr Ross had authorised an additional storey without seeking approval from the UGC, which therefore restricted its contribution to 70 per cent of the final cost. To meet the outstanding balance, the university virtually depleted its building reserve, and in 1958 Principal Taylor indicated that it could accept the building expansion programme of the late 1950s and early 1960s only on the condition that 100 per cent funding was provided by the UGC, so confirming the directional role of the Committee. Even the recurrent grant could be used as a mechanism for guiding the universities; although it was given as a block sum, theoretically for the recipient institution to disburse as it saw best, it was apparent that using money for projects which had not received the blessing of the UGC could provoke retaliatory action at the next quinquennial allocation. The elaborate care taken by the UGC to find the right phrasing to indicate the full extent of its opposition to Aberdeen's engineering proposals of 1950–1 reveals an awareness on both sides of the powers of the Committee.[2] As the recurrent grant from the Committee of £1 million formed 79 per cent of Aberdeen's total income in 1961–2, as against 46 per cent in 1938–9, the leeway for manoeuvre independent of the UGC had been steeply reduced.

A further aspect of government policy in the pre-Robbins era which was to have profound implications for universities was the acceptance of the Anderson Committee's report of 1960 on student grants. This committee, on which Professor Wright played an important role, swept away the system of numerically restricted and financially stringent student scholarships run by local authorities and instead put the case for generous grants financed by the government to be available to *all* students who had secured a place at university. When Robbins subsequently argued that all who were fit to go to university should be able to do so, the Anderson

proposals became instrumental in enabling students to take up the opportunity. But a side-effect was the final elimination of any significant con-
tributory role in financing students on the part of either the university
bursaries or the Carnegie Trust; the state henceforth financed both the
universities and the students to a very large extent.

The ten years from 1963 to 1973 formed a golden age for British universities. The Robbins Committee report accelerated the growth in student
numbers already set in motion, calling for a rise from around 116,000 in
1962–3 to 218,000 a decade later, and for 1980–1 it looked for 246,000
university places. To facilitate this dramatic advance, the Treasury made
available large sums for capital expenditure, and the UGC unpre-
cedentedly reopened the quinquennial allocation to incorporate these
additional sums. The main share of the decade's growth in numbers
was borne by older universities, and Aberdeen played a prominent part,
probably outstripping the other older Scottish universities in its growth
rate; certainly by 1970 its student population was almost double that of
St Andrews, whereas ten years earlier they had been of roughly similar
size. At the UGC's prompting, the university agreed to bring forward
from 1973–4 to 1967–8 the target of 4,500 which it had accepted in 1960;
in 1970–1, 8,180 became the agreed total for 1976–7. The Thatcher White
Paper of 1972 put university student numbers for 1980–1 at 10 per cent
over the Robbins' figure, and so in 1973, 10,500 was settled on as Aberdeen's goal for the start of the next decade. Vast sums were pumped into
the university's capital account to meet the building requirements of this
transformation; in the six years from 1964–5 over £9.4 million was paid
in the form of non-recurrent grants, and in these years the non-recurrent
grant ranged between 35 per cent and 95 per cent of the recurrent grant,
whereas in previous and subsequent periods it rarely went above 20 per
cent.

Various reasons for the UGC's apparent preference for Aberdeen are
discussed in the first chapter of this volume. Moreover, there was a strong
feeling in influential circles (e.g. the SED's evidence to Robbins) that
Edinburgh and Glasgow should not grow too far beyond their existing
size, and that any rapid growth should be in Aberdeen or St Andrews.
But Aberdeen had advantages over St Andrews: it had a better 'mix' of
disciplines, particularly its strong science faculty, which was the sector
Robbins and the UGC were striving to develop ahead of arts. The city of
Aberdeen was sufficiently large to cope with the various demands of an
expanded university, while St Andrews was perhaps too small; certainly
Aberdeen might require less university-built residential accommodation

than St Andrews. Aberdeen had already embarked on a building programme in which the science subjects predominated, because of the flight
from Marischal. These building plans were, again, easy to adjust to provide
for more science students. Aberdeen had skilfully stressed the ready availability of land at Old Aberdeen, so the prospects of speedy completion of
projects and of an attractive, compact campus may have helped sway the
UGC. Probably too, the university's efficient buildings office, led from
1957 by the redoubtable Mr Kelman, impressed the Grants Committee.
Certainly in the late 1950s, the UGC was full of praise for the university's
success in reducing the cost of the Natural Philosophy Building. Mr
Kelman was astute in dealings with the UGC, always alert to finding
economies, and rarely let a building fall behind its completion date.
Whatever the factors behind the UGC's attitude to Aberdeen in the 1960s,
the enlarged target it set in 1972 stemmed from its decision that
Scottish universities should enjoy greater growth in order to ensure
equal opportunities throughout Britain for students to enter higher
education.

    In its survey of the 1962–7 quinquennium, the UGC explained that in
order to ensure that the university sector did not grow in a random and
inefficient manner, the committee was assuming greater powers to direct
and co-ordinate from the centre, and also to set the general strategy. In
particular it strove to ensure that universities did not waste public money
by extravagance; it saw the building programme as the means to shape
individual universities; and it claimed to have taken the initiative in
planning for the optimum provision in subjects like biology, agriculture
and audio-visual aids. While there is much truth in these pointers to a
more *dirigiste* role being assumed by the UGC, Aberdeen's experience
suggests this was an uneven process.

    Firm decisions were indeed handed down by the committee: in March
1967 it firmly squashed a new proposal by the university wholly to
separate its engineering courses from Robert Gordon's. Over the building
programme, seen by the committee itself as the lynch pin of its control
over university development, the UGC seems in the early part of the
decade to have been rather passive, generally acquiescing in Aberdeen's
submissions.[3] By early 1968, however, the UGC stressed that the con-
sequential implications for finance and building work of proposed academic developments should be clearly stated, a trend reinforced by the
building capacity survey carried out a couple of years later. The power of
the Grants Committee in this area was demonstrated markedly in April
1972. When Principal Wright talked of reaching only 7,000 places instead
of the 8,180 target sought by the UGC, the committee's chairman, Sir
Kenneth Berrill, stressed that the funding of the new [Edward Wright]
Arts Building would stop, but the Library and the administration block

would not be hampered. The upshot was that Aberdeen adjusted its figures to come nearer to the UGC's desired target.

The recurrent grants awarded to Aberdeen seem generous in relation to the actual expenditure levels being reached: in the 1960s the university's annual surplus frequently exceeded £100,000 and in 1965–6 it totalled over £180,000. This was about 6 per cent of total income, double the average for both Scotland and Britain. Some of this surplus went on capital expenditure, some to reserve funds, and some to promoting developments over which the UGC's control may have been slender. Of a predicted surplus in 1966–7 of £160,000, the Court allocated £100,000 to be distributed over such heads of expenditure as additional staff, library, departmental grants and sporting facilities.

The firm guidance claimed by the UGC in co-ordinating subject developments clearly applied (beneficially for Aberdeen) in the reduction of agriculture teaching in Great Britain. Of the three Scottish university departments, Glasgow was chosen for closure. But in biology it was perhaps less coherent. The Court minutes report that at the quinquennial visitation of December 1965, Sir John Wolfenden told the University Court that Aberdeen might well consider developing certain areas, specifically citing 'the biological sciences and fields of demographic study'. Acting on this heavy hint, the academic planning mechanism of the university began to move. In June 1966, however, the UGC's minute of the visitation reached the university, which then learned that while the Court records had Wolfenden referring to biological sciences as fit for development, the UGC's account (which is always the official version) stated that he had identified sociological sciences. A hurried phone call to the committee elicited a letter stating that the balance of evidence in the Grants Committee office confirmed his use of the word 'sociological' but suggesting that both sociological and biological science were suitable fields of development for Aberdeen.[4]

Before considering the difficulties of the 1970s, it may be appropriate to examine a complicating factor in relationships between Aberdeen and the state, namely the impact of the Scottish Office on Scottish universities. There was a tradition of closer state involvement with universities north of the border than in England, typified by a succession of commissions of enquiry in the nineteenth century. The culmination was the 1889 Commission, whose report formed the basis for legislation which modernised the administration and curriculum of all four ancient universities.

In the twentieth century this influence was maintained in a number of ways. The Secretary of State made an annual grant under the 1908 Education (Scotland) Act to the Scottish universities. In 1945–6 Aberdeen received £15,000, a figure raised in 1958–9 to £17,000. But whereas in 1945 this constituted over 7 per cent of total income, by the later date it was a mere 2 per cent. Nevertheless, this contribution justified a continuing interest and involvement by St Andrews House in Scottish university matters.

There were three departments at St Andrews House which were closely involved with matters affecting Aberdeen University, although for one of them—the Home and Health Department—the archival records are barren. The other two departments were politically and administratively heavyweights and on occasion appear to have intervened to try to shape university developments. The SED, a powerful and self-confident department which appointed an assessor to the UGC, clearly had an interest, in part because of the Scottish all-graduate secondary teaching profession, and in both the immediate post-war years and the 1960s it probably gave a boost to the case for raising student numbers, as it was worried about shortfalls in entrants to teaching. The SED also had a stronger interest in technological education than its English equivalent as it had direct control of the Central Institutions, of whose achievements the department was very proud, whereas in England local authorities, and not the central government, were administratively responsible for the Colleges of Advanced Technology. So when Aberdeen University proposed in 1950–1 to sever its links in engineering with Robert Gordon's and go on its own, the SED lobbied the UGC vigorously, particularly through two prominent Scottish businessmen, Sir Andrew McCance of Colvilles and Sir Murray Stephen the shipbuilder, who sat on the Technology Sub-committee. The sub-committee was unanimously hostile to the university's case, as was the full UGC, and it is difficult to know if the SED's intervention played any part.[5] In its evidence to Robbins, there are hints of continuing SED suspicions of elitism and non-cooperation on the part of universities where involvement with Central Institutions is concerned. Certainly the blighting of Aberdeen's venture into engineering, which held back growth for about 20 years, meant that when expansion came in the 1970s, it was not at a financially propitious time for launching costly new subjects.

The Scottish Agriculture Department (DAFS) also carried considerable political clout. It had been unhappy at the separation in the late 1940s of the university's agriculture department from the North of Scotland College of Agriculture, and had urged the UGC to withhold a grant for the purchase of Tillycorthie teaching farm, which would have had to be funded out of the university's own resources. The re-marriage of the college and the university between 1959 and 1962 was substantially brought about by the good offices of DAFS, which stalled the college's desire to build on the

Craibstone site, and instead encouraged a joint funding of shared premises at Old Aberdeen, somewhat against the wishes of the college governors. This may well have been a fateful decision, for it is possible that DAFS backing may have helped the university department survive in the reduction in departments recommended by the Bosanquet Report of 1964, which brought about the closure of agriculture teaching at Glasgow University. Perhaps, too, there may have been some benign DAFS influence on the UGC's decision a few years later to keep forestry at Aberdeen, but close it at Edinburgh.

Of course, one can trace the role of government into ever more rarefied areas, but there may be substance to the feeling voiced in the 1970s that the SED, by encouraging a brisk increase in the number of students in non-university institutions of higher education in Aberdeen, exacerbated the university's student accommodation crisis. Whereas the university felt some sort of obligation to ensure decent accommodation was available for its students, the SED-controlled bodies seemed to feel less need, so the student housing market was swamped by heavy demand. The decision by the university that it was necessary to build residences created a major financial difficulty for the whole of the 1970s.

Although the UGC was uttering distinctly less bullish comments about university finance from the end of the 1960s, and signs of government restiveness at aspects of the university system were already showing before 1973, the extent of the downturn between 1973 and 1981 in the fortunes of the whole sector, of which Aberdeen was one of the most spectacular casualties, was remarkable. A decade of retrenchment and contraction followed 30 years of virtually uninterrupted movement onwards and upwards, and the UGC inevitably bore the brunt of the criticism, firstly for failing to combat this process, and then for applying harsh and regressive policies in an apparently random and secretive manner. It is therefore useful to consider the changing wider environment of this period before condemning the committee out of hand.

At the macro-level, the economic difficulties of the 1970s led governments of both parties to decide that the continuation of all categories of public expenditure at earlier levels was untenable; but this does not explain why universities were hit especially hard. Here, a vital factor was the loss of confidence by the government in the benefits to economic growth which had been promised by Robbins (although this had not been the main ground of that committee's case for expanding higher education). In a context where universities were viewed less favourably, it became apparent that the system of state funding was open to pressure at two key points within the bureaucratic process. Firstly, it has been argued that the DES tended to do poorly in resisting expenditure cuts imposed by the Treasury because it had a low position in the Whitehall power structure;

it was numerically small, not many high-fliers were to be found in it, and it had few very effective or long-lasting Secretaries of State (apart from Crosland and Thatcher) to defend it. Then the UGC may well have suffered by being transferred in 1963 from the Treasury to the DES. While in the former, it had direct access to the heart of the government spending system, but in the DES it had to compete with more politically effective elements (notably local authorities) for the allocation of resources. More-over, the UGC budget constituted about two-thirds of the expenditure under the direct control of the DES, so that it was the prime victim of spending reductions, whereas, when in the Treasury, the UGC absorbed only about 2 per cent of all government expenditure. It was consistent with this altered evaluation of universities that Reg Prentice, as Secretary of State for Education, could claim in 1975 that the exceptionally harsh cutbacks recently imposed on them were justified because they had the most 'fat' within the whole area of education.[6]

The erosion of the UGC's status, the depletion of its battery of instru-ments for influencing universities, and the increasingly direct role in shaping policy taken by the state, all proceeded through the 1970s. The UGC was increasingly seen as weak, because it failed to curb extravagance on the part of universities. The DES, under Crosland in the late 1960s, abandoned the traditional government resistance to scrutiny by par-liamentary committees and agencies of how the universities administered the public funds given to them. Critical reports and hostile questioning by three committees—Public Accounts, Estimates, and Education—along with probing investigations by the Comptroller and Auditor-General, all sapped the UGC's morale and standing. The Treasury harboured a dislike of the quinquennial grant system, which was a longer term financial commitment than that enjoyed by any other arm of government, where three-year rolling horizons were the norm, and in 1974–5 the universities lost this preferential treatment.

The DES also began to be more interventionist in its dealings with the Grants Committee, using a number of devices to weaken the UGC's accepted role as the overseer of university development. In 1972, for the first time, it specified to the UGC the exact size of the student population to be sought, and it also detailed, again for the first time, the divide between arts and science. By adjusting upwards the level of fees paid by overseas students, a favourite ploy used repeatedly in the 1970s, the government removed much of the UGC's ability to influence universities through the recurrent grant. The slashing of the building programme grant—from around £30 million in the early 1970s to under £6 million a few years later—meant that virtually no new building took place, further weakening the UGC's powers to guide universities. The imposition in 1979 of full-cost fee levels for overseas students was carried out unilaterally by the government, underscoring the reduced standing of the UGC. The final twist came with the DES's shift from funding based on student numbers to imposing cash-limit financing, so forcing the draconian measures of 1981. From this analysis, the UGC's problem was that it could no longer perform its traditional 'buffer' role, which had depended on the goodwill and co-operation of both sides: the state had altered its position.

Another argument, however, would hold that many of the acute problems posed by the 1981 measures stemmed from mistakes made by the UGC itself. Thus the committee was guilty of not acting decisively in the early 1970s to impose rationalisation on universities, with the failure to tackle the proliferation of small Russian departments (such as at Aberdeen) being the most cited example. The selectivity procedures of 1981 were so punitive because they had been long postponed and inefficiencies allowed to accumulate unchecked. Some also question whether the subject sub-committee reviews which provided the basis for deciding the 1981 cuts were all conducted in a uniform and thorough manner.

From 1974 until the 1981 cuts, the crises faced by universities arising from reductions in state funding were shared across the board by the UGC, and Aberdeen suffered accordingly, with three major areas most obviously affected. Firstly, the projected size of the university was steadily reduced as the UGC strove to meet falling revenue by cutting student numbers. By 1978 the committee had scaled down the 1980–1 target to 5,800, in contrast to the 10,500 predicted in 1973. Secondly, the university found its high surpluses on annual income falling alarmingly from the mid 1970s. In 1975–6, unspent income (including capital expenditure out of revenue funds) was down to 3 per cent, at the same level as the British average, and soon after the Court was warned of the probability of the university's balances going into the red. A significant cost element was that with sharply reduced UGC financial support for building the student residences so vital for meeting the expansion target, loans had to be raised from the Clydesdale Bank, and the interest paid ate into revenue. However, Aberdeen was less hurt than other institutions by the government's manipulation of overseas fee levels, because the university had a smaller proportion of such students. Nevertheless, the university calculated that the impact of the 1979 fees tariff would be extremely grave. It was likely to produce a cumulative annual deficit of £800,000 and to avert this student numbers would have to be reduced by one-eighth, which in turn would create wider uncertainties about the university's viability. Thirdly, new large-scale building projects came to a virtual halt in the later 1970s. The new library was the only exception to the UGC moratorium, but this itself afforded a perfect illustration of the new, uncertain environment. In January 1977, the committee announced that Aberdeen Library would be one of the very few new buildings in the entire university system to be given a capital grant that year. Yet subsequent tightening in central funding meant that the actual release of cash was protracted over several years. In 1979 the UGC decided that it could only meet about two-thirds of the total cost, and moreover in 1980 it forced the unwilling university to reduce the size of the building from four to three bays. The Court not surprisingly complained that the UGC's handling of the whole library building question made realistic academic planning well-nigh impossible.

The imposition of further cuts in state funding which took effect in 1981–2 produced a change of policy by the UGC, in that it applied the reductions selectively. The average reduction, it calculated, was 11 per cent, but the spread of cuts to individual universities ranged from 2 per cent to 40 per cent. Aberdeen faced a fall of 19 per cent in its recurrent grant, which unless immediate drastic action were taken would result in an annual deficit of £3 million. It is not absolutely clear why Aberdeen was given harsh treatment, but several points seem to apply. Firstly, the university had recruited staff ahead of actual student growth, so when the cuts were applied in the mid 1970s, it was over-staffed and therefore had high unit costs. This problem had been recognised by the university itself in 1975–6, but with tenure there was little it could do to reduce staffing levels. Another factor identified by the UGC itself was student demand, and Aberdeen's difficulty in reaching even the reduced targets given to it in the mid and later 1970s by the committee may have been influential. Here the difficulties encountered by Aberdeen in reaching its target for medical students, one of only three universities identified by the committee in 1980 to be falling behind, may have carried weight. Moreover, the committee wished to protect science subject areas, but Aberdeen was drifting by 1978 from its nominal arts : science ratio of 49 : 51 to an actual 53.5 : 46.5. The persistence of the acute accommodation problem which so preoccupied the university throughout the early 1970s may have been a lesser factor. It also seems to be the case that the allocation to universities was more closely tied to student numbers than in the past, when various unquantifiable elements were involved. Aberdeen may have been a beneficiary of the older calculation. The UGC also stressed its desire to protect the science research base: Aberdeen had a relatively low share of its revenue coming from research grants—about 7 per cent in 1980–1, against 12 per cent for Great Britain as a whole. It is difficult to see Aberdeen as a casualty of a failure on the part of the UGC to appreciate the peculiarities of the Scottish university system as some have claimed, since most other Scottish universities were not so badly treated.

Whether the university could have escaped the difficulties of 1981 by diversifying its income and becoming less dependent on the state is not easy to answer. At 79 per cent of total income, Aberdeen's Exchequer grant was identical to the Scottish average, and only 3 per cent above the British. The Carnegie Trust, so important before 1939, although still making quinquennial allocations, could only offer about £50,000 per annum, small beer by 1980–1, when the Exchequer grant exceeded £11 million. Again, personal benefactors like Lord Cowdray and Sir Thomas Jaffrey, who between the wars had almost single-handedly financed the founding of chairs, were no longer present. Industry was an obvious new source of income, and in 1967 the UGC had urged all universities to look to business for more support. But as both Principal Taylor and Principal Wright had pointed out at different times, Aberdeen did not have the sort of business and industrial presence enjoyed by most other university cities. Yet the failure to exploit the possibilities offered by North Sea oil is puzzling, especially when other institutions seem to have succeeded. There are almost signs of what might be termed a 'state dependency culture' here, for the university seems to have looked to the UGC to do more in the mid 1970s to help it move into oil related work, with a low expectation of much direct aid from the oil industry itself.[7]

Since 1945, Aberdeen, like all universities, had become increasingly reliant on the central government for funding. So long as the interests of universities and state remained broadly congruent, the UGC could operate to the advantage of both. However when the state, which as paymaster was the dominant partner in the relationship, changed its policy, universities found it hard to adjust and the UGC was no longer able to perform its role as intermediary. Blame for this disorderly breakdown can be ascribed to all three sides. The universities were slow to sense the altered climate of opinion in government, as their disdainful response to Mrs Williams' Thirteen Points showed; the UGC seemed unable to give firm direction when the universities most needed it, and then over-adjusted in an erratic and secretive way; the state held unrealistic assumptions about the speed with, and extent to which universities could alter their long term planning. But it is salutary to recall that for most of the period under review Aberdeen University responded positively on the whole to the demands made of it by the state, and that normally the UGC warmly supported the university in its schemes. It remains an open question whether the new dispensation in force since 1981 will be as successful in achieving the high academic standards attained in the preceding period through close collaboration between the state and the university.

Commentary to Chapter 7

A View from the UGC

JOHN CANNON

It is a curious experience to sit and listen to Dr Hutchison's excellent paper. I have always wondered why Burns wrote, 'O wad some Pow'r the giftie gie us / to see oursels as others see us!'. Most of us would hate it—a very disagreeable power to have. I think of my friends on the UGC—Tom and Douglas and Sidney—genial to a fault, devoted to the higher interests of scholarship, kind to children, generous on flagdays—and hardly recognise them as these grim-faced, meddlesome men, perpetually lecturing and reproaching institutions. Indeed, I fell awondering what we had been doing in my years on UGC, and decided that, among all the twists and turns of tactics, there were two guiding principles: the preservation of the unit of resource, and the maintenance, as far as possible, of the block grant. Neither of them at first sight sounds a very fascinating objective—but the first means good standards of teaching, good standards of research, decent conditions of service and a reasonable career prospect for staff, while the second means some degree of independence for universities against the persistently encroaching power of the state. One could think of worse principles.

The sub-title of Dr Hutchison's paper might well have been 'Whatever happened to liberalism?' The concept of a series of checks and balances on the power of the state is not much regarded in modern days, and much of the paper is a sad tale of how the buffer, which the UGC was designed to be, was first squeezed flat, and then discarded. For it is clear that towards its end, UGC was being both pushed into a more interventionist stance *vis-à-vis* the universities, while its own advice to government was increasingly ignored.

I want to throw two points into our discussion this evening. Why did it happen? Could it be reversed? And, perhaps, should it be reversed?

Dr Hutchison has provided us with many clues to the growing disenchantment with higher education—a faltering economic performance, heavy alternative demands on the public purse (particularly those of health), and some feeling of disappointment and resentment that the great expansion of the 1960s had not produced all that was hoped for. I suppose it is possible that there was some over-investment and some two or three universities too many were established—though you will not expect me to suggest which two or three.

There is one factor I throw into the discussion, though I do not know how important it is, and I hope it does not suggest paranoia on my part. But I am struck by the respect—even affection—which most graduates seem to feel for their old universities, as against the downright hostility which others seem to feel for the universities of this country. I wonder whether the student troubles of the 1960s and early 1970s did not do quite disproportionate damage to the public image of the universities? You will say, of course, that our own troubles were slight compared with those of America, France or Germany—and I would agree. I think that student unrest in this country was very sensibly handled and very moderate in tone. But there has been very little tradition of student involvement in politics in Britain—it is a commonplace on the continent—and its arrival was not much welcomed by the general public.

One of the main themes of Dr Hutchison's paper has been the increased dependence since 1945 on government funding, and it is an avowed object of the present government to reduce that dependence. It is not easy to quarrel with it as a principle—we all like to run our own affairs. But the limitations on outside funding are not always appreciated. One alternative source of funding is, of course, to recruit foreign students, and most of us are busy trying to do that. But there is not much point in labouring to reduce our dependence upon the British government in order to finish up dependent on the Algerian government or the Malaysian government. It is all very well to preach the merits of marketing. Lots of people can play that game, and foreign governments are well aware that their students represent a marketable—and therefore a negotiable—commodity. We are told to look to industry for help, and universities have been very successful in increasing their income from that source. But it is usually ear-marked and not necessarily for what would have been the universities' own priority. It is, as we all know, much easier to raise in some areas than others. It is not freely disposable income and there is a serious danger that it could distort the balance of what we study. I must also confess to feeling rather sorry for industrialists, though I write my begging letters as we all do. They are already being implored to support ballet, orchestras, local football teams, youth schemes. I suppose at times it does occur to them that their primary function is to make profits for their shareholders. Can they really take on the universities as well?

I hope I have said enough to introduce a few more points for discussion. I am afraid that I have certainly said enough to make it clear how old-fashioned I am. In the last analysis I regard higher education as a national responsibility, which the government has to accept. After all, we do not leave national defence to private enterprise—with businesses clubbing together to buy an Aberdeen tank or a Bristol missile. Is not education of equal importance?

Chapter 8

Summaries and Signposts

JOHN HARGREAVES

The preceding papers, and the lively discussions which they inspired, point those concerned with the health of our universities towards many uncompleted tasks. There are needs for more historical research, and for more attempts to record the oral testimony of participants; for it became clear that universities are no better than other bodies in preserving the written records of their activities. There are needs for more systematic comparisons; since most of the experiences chronicled here could be paralleled in other British universities, it remains necessary to explain why Aberdeen became particularly vulnerable to new government policies after 1981. And many will surely feel a need to reflect on the relevance of those experiences to problems currently confronting Aberdeen and other centres of learning. This chapter, besides reviewing discussions in the seminar and recording some of the thoughtful commentaries prepared for us, will tentatively raise a few signposts towards future studies.

These papers show Aberdeen University endeavouring to marry its responsibilities, traditions, and established routines as the university of northern Scotland to the wider academic frontiers and social objectives of post-war Britain. Since 1945, public expenditure on universities in the United Kingdom has risen to levels previously unimaginable; in return universities have been expected to undertake more intensive programmes of research (which were in turn to contribute to the development of the national economy); to provide access to higher education for much larger sections of the population; and (at least until recently) to conduct that education in an atmosphere of broadly liberal scholarship and academic community.

As these papers suggest, Aberdeen's response to these three demands, like that of any other university, has been variable. Perhaps the most difficult adjustment has been to the new environment of research. Although the university staff has always included distinguished scholars and scientists (more Nobel laureates were associated with the university in the pre-war than in the post-war years), postgraduate students were commonly directed to other centres. Since 1945 this situation has changed dramatically. Although qualitative assessment of the total research achievement is quite beyond the capacity of this (and probably any) author, according to measurements used by the UGC since 1981 it has not been distinguished. But over 10 per cent of the student body is now engaged in postgraduate study, though this proportion is still below the national average.[1]

With regard to access, the myth, and to a lesser degree the reality, is that Aberdeen and other Scottish universities have always been more open to talent than those in England.[2] During the 1950s the belief that the regional 'pool of talent' was being fully drained may have somewhat delayed expansion, but in the 'Robbins period' the university consistently claimed to welcome qualified students of all social origins. How far its definitions of qualification may have in practice restricted access is another question; as was pointed out in discussion, the social and ethnic origins of the post-war student body still await analysis. Most enthusiastic expansionists were also anxious to improve access for those without standard school backgrounds, and it is the author's impression that Aberdeen was more ready than some other universities to admit mature students in the 1960s and 1970s. But it did not undertake the provision of formal Access courses until 1984.

If these were the intentions of the university, how are historians or policy-makers to assess its actual performance? Economic criteria are fashionable, and two specialised commentators congratulated Alex Kemp and Sandra Galbraith on their pioneering attempt to calculate the university's impact on the economy of Grampian Region, both as a spending and employing body and as a provider of skilled labour. *Max Gaskin*, after suggesting that the economic impact of the university might be more meaningfully assessed within the more restricted area of greater Aberdeen (where most of the relevant expenditure took place), went on to raise wider issues concerning regional economic performance:

> From a narrow point of view the role of the university as a supplier of labour to the region is that it reduces one important expenditure leakage; it supplies an important service, higher education, which some intending participants in the local labour market would otherwise obtain elsewhere.

On this restricted view of what the university does its presence within the region simply internalises one important service which would otherwise be 'imported' (and which is 'exported' in the case of those of its students whom it attracts from other parts of the country). To take this view of the matter is to say, in effect, that the economic significance of the university can indeed be totally summarised in the multiplier model. To avoid this position, or at least to explore whether it is avoidable, one would need to consider the impact of the university on the economic performance of the region.

To this difficult area of enquiry there are perhaps two lines of approach. Following on from the analysis of graduates in regional employment one might consider such questions as:

—does the university, as a supplier of educated labour, improve the structure and effectiveness of the local labour market?
—does it thereby improve the performance of local industry and services?
—does it make the region more attractive to incoming industry?

These are very difficult, largely qualitative, questions, to which one cannot expect clear-cut answers. But their exploration might shed some light, and could be a valuable enquiry in itself; and Aberdeen, geographically placed as it is, offers more feasible opportunities for such a study than most universities.

The second line of approach would consider the university as a supplier of research, special teaching services, consultancies and so forth to the local economy. Part of the *raison d'être* of AURIS and similar developments of the last ten years was the view that the university had a duty to share any relevant expertise it had to assist industry and the public sector, and so contribute to the performance of the economy, both regional and national.

The second commentator, *Edward Cunningham* of the Scottish Development Agency, also asked broader questions about the role of universities in their local community:

The answer, he suggested, must be concerned both with quality (intellectual quality: the quality of teaching, research, innovation, and skill), and with the mechanisms whereby a university transfers its expertise into local society. While conceding the difficulty of such a complex assessment, Cunningham posed the question of how Aberdeen University's performance compared with that of other universities. He argued that one had to go beyond the usual definition of the function of a university as the pursuit of knowledge: the university must also be a centre of creativity and development, providing usable research and 'prime movers' to lead society. He asked what such contributions Aberdeen made to the regional economy, and how far these were a proper function of the university: should university education be a manufacturing operation—raw goods in, finished goods out—or should enhancing the local community be a subsidiary function?

Cunningham offered two propositions concerning a university's contribution to local needs. Firstly, part of the curriculum must be relevant
to the hereafter (e.g. engineering courses should be practical as well as
theoretical); secondly, local needs should be reflected in curricula (e.g the
oil industry should have access to university research). He challenged the
seminar to say what, in the way of creativity, development and research,
Aberdeen University had brought to the region since Thomas Reid's
Philosophy of Common Sense. It was necessary to investigate how far, in
more recent periods, Aberdeen had made intellectual property and research
available for use outside the confines of the university, and how far its
curricula were related to local needs (not only those of oil, but of industries
like agriculture, fisheries, and tourism). He suggested that the com-
mercialisation of expertise, in the form of joint ventures between the
university and industry, or of contractual research, was an important
element, and enquired about the success of recent initiatives like AURIS
and the Science Park.

Commenting on the trend to see universities as playing prominent roles
internationally, nationally and locally, Cunningham maintained that the
origin and proper role of universities were primarily regional, and that the
imperial period had tended to distract them from this.

While the paper of Kemp and Galbraith represents an original and
overdue attempt to measure certain contributions by the university to the
region, many of its most important influences can hardly be quantified.
The people of Grampian would find it difficult to place a cash value on
the university's contribution to their health. But Roy Weir shows that the
Medical School's unusually deep and long-established involvement in
regional health care seems to have led some of its departments, during its
post-1960 expansion, to concentrate on developing its clinical services at
the expense of its reputation for research. Though Weir can list some
notable research achievements, it was agreed in discussion that opportunities were missed to make greater contributions to the progress of
medical science, including studies of the health of local populations. The
high incidence of multiple sclerosis in north-eastern Scotland was cited as
one challenge to which researchers might have responded more positively,
as Sir Dugald Baird had earlier reacted to that of maternal mortality.

John Sewel's paper identifies other areas of public life within which the
university might be expected to provide leadership and be a source of
creative innovation in the region. His preliminary conclusions suggest that
the university should not be complacent about its achievements; but there
are other subjects on which self-assessment might be attempted. In seeking
funds to maintain its Library as a major centre for reference, research and
scholarship the university has laid stress upon its regional responsibilities.
It has indeed built up excellent collections in many fields, and it would be

interesting to measure the extent of their use by staff of the Research Institutes, of Grampian Regional Council, and by others within the region. Many other questions suggest themselves. What contribution is made to local choirs and orchestras by our apparently doomed music department? What has the presence of the university meant to local churches—not simply in the training of ministers but through the activities of educated laity? What have members of the university contributed to the work of the Trades Council, or to post-war developments in the labour movement? More broadly, what substance is there in the feeling, expressed in discussion, that the university in these years became an alien growth within local culture—that it 'lost its regional voice'?

As regards students, Table II in the Statistical Appendix suggests that regional connections have been weakened, but by no means destroyed, by growing perceptions on the part of applicants of the benefits of study away from home. Also the wider range of opportunities available in RGIT has (as with the polytechnics in England) offered attractive alternatives to those seeking higher education within their home region. But the university's student body has remained predominantly Scottish, with Aberdeen increasingly favoured by students from Lothian region in particular; it has continued to contribute to many local activities, cultural and political, and to conduct outstandingly successful Charity campaigns. The influence of a more cosmopolitan staff may have weakened the 'regional voice'; but one shrewd commentator expressed the view that the most condescending attitudes towards local culture were often those of locally born teachers who had studied at Oxbridge.

Sewel echoes Gaskin in suggesting that regional contributions through teaching and research deserve closer study than has been feasible within the scope of the current exercise. To complement Kemp's study of graduate employment we need to ask how far university initiatives, in both full-time and continuing education, have been directed to serve local needs. Sewel is surely right to suggest that there has been more adaptation to changing structures in the professions (law, accountancy, social work) than to the claims of industry or business management. Yet the abolition in 1949 of the Bachelor of Commerce degree, over protests from the Aberdeen Chamber of Commerce, is too readily cited to support this view. Although for twelve years following its inception in 1920–1 this degree appears to have been rather successful in preparing students for business careers, after the depression of the 1930s numbers declined sharply. Against an average of over ten graduates a year in the 1920s, in 1937 there were three; there was one in each of the next three years, and no students at all after 1940.[3] So the course was hardly justifiable by modern criteria of cost effectiveness. All the same, the decision not to persist with it did reflect a general post-war belief that universities should concentrate on the education of an open and meritocratic academic and professional elite. If Sir Thomas Taylor believed that such practical studies could more properly be pursued in such places as Robert Gordon's he was not alone in such attitudes; most vice-chancellors of the period linked their insistence on the maintenance of academic quality and standards with implicit assumptions about a division of academic labour within what came to be known as the binary system. Most universities which continued to offer a B Com degree seem, under the influence of the Clapham Committee, to have emphasised 'research into economic and social questions' rather than practical business studies; and courses in Aberdeen were certainly not exempt from such a trend.

To answer the commentators' questions about the regional relevance of university research is hardly simpler than to assess its quality. Sewel, a survivor of the Institute for the Study of Sparsely Populated Areas established in 1973, lists many examples of 'intellectual engagement' by social scientists with problems of northern Scotland. Max Gaskin recalled how on his appointment to the chair of political economy in 1965 he redirected his research efforts towards regional economics, and his report of 1969 was seen as a timely response to the 'stirring of industrial interest' which preceded the oil boom. Nor was Gaskin the only person to feel such an obligation. Long standing links between natural scientists and neighbouring research institutes, the marriage of the College of Agriculture with the university department, the evident local opportunities in forestry, all tended in the same direction. As regards industry, regional engagement was perhaps less strong; the terms of the complex partnership with Robert Gordon's which the UGC insisted on maintaining may have meant that this came more naturally to those working in RGIT. Nevertheless it was notable that the much publicised charge of failure to perceive the 'potentially strategic significance' of oil[4] was not endorsed by Edward Cunningham of the Scottish Development Agency, and that the Scottish Office commissioned a major study of the economic impact of North Sea oil as early as 1972.

Some critics of the university's relations with industry may be suggesting that the university's tendency during this period to seek public rather than industrial sponsorship for research reflects what is fashionably called a 'dependency culture'. But this was essentially a principled stand; most academics regarded the autonomous intermediaries created by the state as their proper and most enlightened patrons. Principals Taylor and Wright in turn decided not to launch general public appeals for funds for fear of weakening the responsibility for expansion which the UGC had deliberately assumed. Before the end of the period the dangers of dependence on a single source of patronage were becoming more evident; sociologists wasted valuable time and much nervous energy in discussing with the SSRC their plans to study the social impact of North Sea oil.[5] Yet it was surely reasonable to doubt whether, on such a subject, the oil companies would prove disinterested patrons?

A more radical rejoinder to the charge that the university has been inadequately engaged with the problems of its region was made by *Gerard Rochford*:

> Rejecting Sewel's emphasis on the task of a university to produce a work-force for society, Rochford contended that its primary function is the pursuit of truth. If it neglects this, it will die. The most important departments in any university are thus those of philosophy, mathematics, and theology: service to the community is always secondary to the pursuit of truth. Nevertheless medicine was a good example of a field where both purposes could be served. Rochford questioned Weir's view that health care 'merely reflects' and is largely determined by society; he felt, for example, that the domination of psychiatry by drug treatment was not consumer-led, nor was the development of abortion services. He particularly felt that the medical faculty had not given sufficient prominence to medical ethics.
>
> Rochford felt that Aberdeen University had enriched the local com-munity in many ways, citing culture, religion, voluntary work, and sport; and that it had been penalised for this by those who had recently sat in judgement upon it. He regretted the tendency to demean elements in the local culture, paradoxically, even among those who felt the strongest local pride. All the same, he insisted, in response to the charge of a lost 'regional voice', that universities should pay more attention to dialectics than to dialect.

Several speakers took issue from another point of view with Cun-ningham's suggestion that the imperial period had distracted universities from pursuit of their proper regional roles, insisting that responsibilities to the region, the nation, and the international community were and remain essentially complementary. Much work in the applied biological sciences, and in such social sciences as agricultural economics, is no less relevant to development in Asia and Africa than in Scotland, and *John Raeburn* was particularly insistent that the university still has great oppor-tunities, and responsibilities, in such directions. Nor are the benefits all on one side; several speakers testified that comparative or complementary experience derived from work in quite different environments could exercise creative influence upon the direction of research and teaching in Aberdeen. If the African Studies Group and the Institute of South-East Asian Biology have operated on more modest scales than area centres established elsewhere, each may claim to have contributed to the advance of useful knowledge in their respective disciplines. Many also emphasised the benefit which the Aberdeen academic community has derived from its growing component of overseas members during the period (although fluctuations in student numbers suggested by Table I were accompanied by as yet uncharted changes in region of origin, reflecting growing government insistence on treating foreign students as a source of university revenue rather than an intrinsically desirable extension of a university's work). Norwegian medicals recruited during the 1950s, British Council scholars from Africa and Asia during the 1950s and 1960s, exchange students from Europe and the USA, were all seen as having contributed positively to university life in Aberdeen. There seemed to be wide agreement that academic responsibilities to region and nation can only be discharged within an international context, and that a growing consciousness of this context has been a powerful antidote to that cosy parochialism which many sensed during the early years of the period.

Cosiness and parochialism were certainly terms repeatedly used, if somewhat imprecisely, notably during discussion of Colin McLaren's paper. Applied to certain emphases in teaching or research, they may simply register the degree of commitment to regional responsibilities. They may also however be applied to the value systems and intellectual horizons within which senior members of the university live and work, and these seem impossible to measure. It may be that parochial outlooks are encouraged by geographical isolation; but during this period the university (and the Carnegie Trust) deliberately increased provision for academic travel, and it would be difficult to demonstrate that common room conversation was consistently more parochial than elsewhere. It was however suggested that on important matters of national university policy Aberdeen was less able than universities nearer to London to sense and respond to significant changes in the political climate.

On another view of parochialism, the student community might be judged to have been abnormally introverted; but it is difficult to establish norms of public awareness. The very modest signs of rebelliousness during the revolutionary year of 1968 were cited as evidence of exceptional parochialism; but a recent history of St Hugh's College, Oxford, suggests even greater docility in that supposedly cosmopolitan society.[6] Sport, drama, music, conviviality, are always strong competitors with student politics. But many reminiscences made clear that international issues, most consistently the scandal of apartheid, were rarely forgotten in Aberdeen.

Another possible index of cosiness might be found in relations between staff and students; testimonies from both sides suggested that, particularly during the early years of this period, these became closer than formerly. *Charles Gimingham* pointed out how the great increase of younger lecturing staff made social interaction easier than in pre-war years, when a professorial invitation could be a daunting occasion for shy north-eastern students. (Generational change in both professorial and student attitudes was also observed!) The extension of fieldwork and excursions, overseas as well as in the United Kingdom, provided excellent opportunities for contacts between students and their teachers, especially in natural sciences and geography, while many other departments began to arrange reading parties at The Burn or, after 1960, at Tarradale House. Such contacts were also facilitated by the growing student preference for Honours, rather than Ordinary, degree courses. At more formal levels, new provisions of the 1970s for student participation in academic government reflected general movements within British universities rather than any circumstances peculiar to Aberdeen; that they were implemented so smoothly is due not only to the quality of student leadership but, as David Strachan and others emphasised, to the influence of Sir Edward Wright. His humane attitudes created an atmosphere where students could feel themselves part of the academic community, always assured of just and sympathetic treatment.

If the machinery of university government adapted itself well to the growing demand for student participation, there was general support for Jennifer Carter's view that its most serious failure was in devising adequate machinery to involve the Senatus (and so the bulk of the academic community) in planning the allocation of resources during the process of expansion. One experienced commentator compared the planning structures of the university unfavourably with those at RGIT. During the 1960s there was great pressure to proceed with building programmes essential for the expansion of the basic undergraduate disciplines; possibly too little time was taken to look further ahead. Moreover future needs in arts and science were largely dependent on unpredictable decisions by students, whose large freedom of choice was highly valued in the Scottish educational system. This freedom extended to the option of changing faculties; students applying to transfer from science to arts contributed to repeated failures to meet the proportions of science students recommended by the UGC.

In the 1970s, when the immediate pressure of students actually requiring instruction was replaced by the UGC's insistence on preparing for great future increases, it seems clear in retrospect that more thoughtful collegiate planning was needed. But by this time academic departments, whether professorially or collegially led, had become accustomed to taking the initiative in planning their own expansion. It was natural that they should press for resources to enable them to continue and develop the excellent work which they believed they were doing; and so long as finance was being generously provided by the UGC, faculties and Senatus tended simply to approve combined shopping lists, selected in accordance with prevailing student demand. This procedure did not prevent innovations in anticipation of national needs (e.g. computing, accountancy, medical physics, microbiology, social work); but it did make planning much more difficult and painful as the resources available became more constrained.

Such self-criticism did not remove the widespread feeling that the university, having been pressed towards unrealistic targets of expansion by the UGC, had been badly treated by that body since 1981. The phrase 'the UGC got it wrong' was frequently heard. But behind the criticisms of particular UGC decisions lay questions about the difficulty of respecting academic liberties while undertaking central planning of a nationally funded system. *Willis Pickard*, commenting on the opening discussion of strategies of expansion, suggested two alternative lessons:

> 1. All central planning is bound to be wrong. Institutions should determine their own pace of change because only they know best. That in present-day terms is roughly what Sir Graham Hills, principal of Strathclyde University, is saying: universities should seek their own fortunes and map out their own destinies. Unfortunately, that ignores the financial facts of life. Universities are and always will be dependent on government for the bulk of their money. As taxpayers should we dissent from that?

> 2. If, therefore, central planning must continue in one form or another, should we be looking at the mechanism itself? The UGC, we all agree in Aberdeen, has got it wrong about this institution since 1981. But there has been an argument which goes like this: all higher education must reduce its spending because the Treasury says so, and in making cuts there must be hard, even invidious decisions. That argument has been used to excuse the harshness, the irrationality of cuts imposed here. But the argument falls down when we learn that the UGC has got it wrong consistently—in good times as well as bad. We must therefore ask ourselves whether the machinery itself is flawed. Can a UGC or its successor body, the Universities Funding Council, based in London, really know or care about the Scottish universities, either when asking them to expand sensibly or to contract rationally and determinedly? It becomes incumbent on those who would keep a British-based organisation for university finance to defend that position in the light of all the evidence. The onus is no longer on those of us who for long have argued the need to re-establish the Scottish dimension and to set up a planning and funding council for the universities and colleges within Scotland.

While Iain Hutchison sheds some light on possible attitudes of Scottish officialdom towards a devolved university system, most of his paper, and of the subsequent discussion introduced by John Cannon's vigorous defence of UGC objectives, focused on the increasing difficulty which such intermediary institutions of state are experiencing in remaining free from control by their government paymaster. On this sector, among others, the frontiers of the state have been moving relentlessly forward since 1979. *John Nisbet* noted how, in the last years of the UGC, its role as 'buffer' changed from that of the universities' protector against government interference to that of reluctant intermediary in the application of government pressure. He thought universities should aim to recapture public confidence in their capacity to plan their own development along lines clearly compatible with national needs. The judiciary, though centrally financed, still remained an effective buffer between the state and the individual; he hoped the universities might still re-establish their claim to similar privilege.

But this discussion took place during the last month of life at the UGC; and Cannon himself, while echoing some of these hopes, seemed none too confident that the new Universities Funding Council will be able to withstand strong pressure from the Thatcherite Leviathan. Since Sir Peter Swinnerton-Dyer undertook to rationalise the university system (with the same improvident zeal that Dr Beeching once directed to the nation's railways) the buffer seems to have been effectively flattened. Those who, while celebrating the achievements of 1945–81, were simultaneously grappling with the last epistles of the UGC, could not fail to notice how the language of 'management' has superseded an older vocabulary, in which such terms as scholarship, learning, academic community, common culture, were more prominent. Universities seem to have been among the victims of a cultural revolution, to which neither they nor the wider British public have ever been asked explicitly to assent.

This volume is about the recent past; but the discussions it records inevitably raised the question of how in the future Aberdeen University may be able to sustain its regional responsibilities, and its inherited academic ideals, against externally determined criteria of national need. It became clear that many features of the university now regarded as weaknesses by cost accountants were formerly widely held to its credit. After the union of King's and Marischal in 1860, the university provided both a broadly liberal education (chiefly for the youth of northern Scotland), and professional training, notably in medicine (used more widely in the service of the British empire). The tendency after 1945 for this balance to tip towards the former side was not confined to Aberdeen; if the Robbins Committee put 'instruction in skills suitable to play a part in the general division of labour' first among the aims of higher education, its other three aims all derived from the liberal tradition recently restated by Moberley.[7] This seminal report legitimised the instinctive belief of many academics that, if qualified students and teachers were left free to pursue those studies which most interested them, the benefits to the nation would justify the expense.

But it was always clear that the expense would be considerable, and the interaction between wider student access and increasingly sophisticated methods of teaching and research brought growing pressures to demonstrate economy and efficiency. An early warning of government concern came from Shirley Williams in 1969, but British universities still felt sufficiently confident of their prestige and popularity to dismiss her questions lightly. When a real tightening of financial constraints came from Margaret Thatcher's government in 1981 it was accompanied by a new ideological insistence that higher education should demonstrate its relevance to immediate needs of the national economy, and by implicit reassessments of educational values which amounted to a cultural revolution directed from above. Our discussions showed that many believe Aberdeen to have been penalised for what it formerly counted among its achievements.

Notes

INTRODUCTION, pp. 1 to 3

1   J R Lucas, 'Historian malgré moi', in L Pompa and W H Dray, eds, *Substance and Form in History* (Edinburgh, 1981), 141.

CHAPTER 1, pp. 4 to 14

References in this chapter to expansion plans are largely based on the minutes of the University Court, in which the more important correspondence with the UGC was incorporated, and on those of the Senatus; most of the relevant dates are indicated in the text. Statistics for Aberdeen University are taken from the annual returns preserved in the university registry; UK comparisons are based on the Robbins Report, PP 1963, xii, Cmnd 2154, *Higher Education; Report of the Committee ... under the Chairmanship of Lord Robbins, 1961–63*, or on the UGC's periodic reports on university development. Academic developments are charted with help of University *Calendars*. I have also drawn on the memories of former colleagues, some of which are formally recorded in the university's oral archive, and am particularly grateful to Professor R V Jones for lending me some of his personal papers. The text has been revised in the light of many helpful contributions to the seminar discussions.

1   T M Taylor, *Speaking to Graduates* (Aberdeen, 1965), 167.
2   R V Jones papers: Speech at opening of Natural Philosophy Building, May 1964.
3   Willis Pickard comments:
    A senior academic at St Andrews University who was deeply involved there during the expansionist era contrasted to me the pace of growth there with that at Aberdeen. He suggested that there may have been several reasons for the more measured pace of expansion in St Andrews— the size of the town, pre-occupation with the effects of the split with Dundee, and possibly the ability of university leaders to keep control of events.
4   PP 1968–9, XLVII, *University Development, 1962–7*, Cmnd 3820, paras 297–8.
5   I am grateful to Iain Hutchison for drawing my attention to relevant tables (46 or 45) in the annual *Educational Statistics*.

CHAPTER 2, pp. 19 to 46

In the preparation of this paper the authors are grateful for the advice and assistance of several university staff, including Mr C A McLaren, University Archivist; Mr M S Martin, Planning Accountant; Mr A Stirling, Financial Accountant; Mr D Haggart, Senior Careers Advisory Officer; and Mr A Wiseman, Administrative Officer. We are grateful for data on student grants received from Mrs M Deveney of the Scottish Education Department. Our greatest debt is to Mr Hector Williams, Computer Programmer/Statistician in the university economics department, who skilfully tabulated the data employed in the study and produced the many charts. We received many useful comments from the discussants and participants at the seminar where we presented our initial findings. We are, of course, responsible for the final product.

1   M Brownrigg, 'The economic impact of a new university', *Scottish Journal of Political Economy*, 23, no.2 (1973), 125.
2   M A Greig, 'Regional multiplier effects in the UK: a comment', *Oxford Economic Papers*, 23, no.2 (1971), 278.
3   M Brownrigg, 127.
4   Fraser of Allander Institute, *The Economic Impact of University Funding Cuts*, Report prepared for the Association of University Teachers (Scotland), May 1988, 48.
5   M Brownrigg, 135.
6   M Brownrigg, 134.
7   J Mackintosh, *Roll of the Graduates of the University of Aberdeen, 1926–1955* (Aberdeen, 1960), and L Donald and W S Macdonald, *Roll of the Graduates of the University of Aberdeen, 1956–1970* (Aberdeen, 1982).

CHAPTER 6, pp. 91 to 103

The minutes of Court and Senatus form the main basis for this chapter. The memories of colleagues and former colleagues, including some recorded in the university's oral archive, have also been most helpful, and I am particularly grateful to Mr T B Skinner for lending me some documentary evidence to supplement his comments. The text has been revised in the light of discussions during the whole seminar series.

1   G C Moodie and R Eustace, *Power and Authority in British Universities* (London, 1974) identify the challenges from students and from non-professorial staff as the two major challenges to traditional authority within British universities.
2   David S Lovejoy, 'Scholarly reminiscences', *William and Mary Quarterly*, 45 (1988), 549.
3   Moodie and Eustace, *Power and Authority*, 206–7.
4   R D Anderson, *The Student Community at Aberdeen 1860–1939*, Quincentennial Studies in the History of the University of Aberdeen (Aberdeen, 1988), 36–41, 88, 101, 106–8.
5   W Douglas Simpson, ed., *The Fusion of 1860: A Record of the Centenary Celebrations and a History of the University of Aberdeen 1860–1960*, Aberdeen University Studies Series, 146 (Edinburgh, 1963), 101–2, 125.
6   R E Tyson and R Shilton, *Aberdeen Association of University Teachers 1921–1971*, npnd [Aberdeen, 1971], 2–3.

7   *Gaudie*, 23 November 1966.
8   The author wishes to state that she has never felt discriminated against, and this was the view also of Professor Elizabeth Fraser when interviewed for the oral archive.
9   A H Halsey and M A Trow, *The British Academics* (London, 1971), 158.
10 *University Statistics 1980* (Universities' Statistical Record, 1981), vol.1, Table 25.

CHAPTER 7, pp. 108 to 119

Most generous financial assistance towards the cost of gathering material for this paper has been given by the British Academy and the Carnegie Trust for the Universities of Scotland. I am grateful for the many suggestions made by participants in the discussion which followed the delivery of this paper. The comments of Professors J Cannon and J Nisbet were particularly helpful.

A Note on Sources
Primary sources consulted at Aberdeen University Library included the Minutes of the Court (printed); the records of Court Committees (U 389); the Minutes of the Finance Committee of the Court (U 842); the subject file on Agriculture (U 803). At the Public Record Office, London, the records of the University Grants Committee, particularly classes UGC 1, 7, 8, 9, were useful. Among the records of the Education and Agriculture Departments of the Scottish Office held in the Scottish Record Office, Edinburgh, classes ED 26 (Education) and AF 70 (Agriculture) had much relevant material.
    The annual reports by the UGC and its quinquennial reviews of university development are all published as Parliamentary Papers. The Robbins Committee Report is indispensable. Three revealing Select Committee Reports are the Estimates Committee (PP 1964–5, VI), the Expenditure Committee (PP 1972–3, XX); the Science and Technology Committee (PP 1974–5, XXXIV).
    Among the secondary literature, J Carswell, *Government and the Universities in Britain* (Cambridge, 1985) is an informative account by an insider, and P Scott, *The Crisis of the University* (London, 1984) is stimulating. Two articles in *Higher Education* are invaluable: G C Moodie, 'Buffer, coupling and broker, reflections on sixty years of the U.G.C.', 12 (1983), 331–47; M Shattock and R O Berdahl, 'The British University Grants Committee, 1919–83: changing relationships with government and universities', 13 (1984), 471–99.
1   Court Finance Committee Minutes, 6 February 1945, AUL, MS U 862/19.
2   The committee veered between three formulations: that it would 'definitely forbid' the proposal; that it was 'not convinced of the desirability of developing' engineering; and that it 'did not think that this development should be carried out'. It opted for the last. UGC Minutes, 26 June 1952, PRO, UGC 1/3.
3   The transcript in Aberdeen University Archives of the interview with Mr Kelman conducted on 3 April 1985 is illuminating, especially pp. 17–19.
4   Aberdeen University, *Minutes of Court*, 8 December 1965, 5 July 1966.
5   Minutes of the University Grants Committee, 27/28 November 1951, 26 June 1952, PRO, UGC 1/3; Technology Sub-Committee Minutes, 13 November 1951, 10 June 1952, PRO, UGC 8/44,53; Scottish Record Office, ED 26/1009 *passim*.

6 *Select Committee on Science and Technology* (PP 1974–5, XXXIV), Q 302.
7 *Select Committee on Science and Technology* (PP 1974–5, XXXIV), Qq 630–9 reveals the views of Professor Whiteman and Principal Wright.

CHAPTER 8, pp. 123 to 134

1 Because of changing categorisation of postgraduate students, it is difficult to establish exact comparisons; but in 1938–9 the 20 PhD students (all in science) constituted under 2 per cent of the student body. This proportion rose to about 3.6 per cent in 1950–1, and to 6.25 per cent in 1960–1. Comparable figures for all UK universities (excluding Education students) were respectively 6.3 per cent, 9.8 per cent, and 13.1 per cent. (*Robbins Report*, App.II, Table 29). In 1980–1 the Aberdeen figure was 10.9 per cent, compared to a UK average of 15.8 per cent (*University Statistics, 1980*, Vol.I, p.36). See also the Note to Table I in the Statistical Appendix.
2 See R D Anderson, *Education and Opportunity in Victorian Scotland* (Oxford, 1983) ,Chs 4, 8, and *The Student Community at Aberdeen 1860–1939* (Aberdeen, 1988), pp.59–60, Tables 7, 10.
3 Figures of employment quoted in M Sanderson, *The Universities and British Industry, 1850–1970* (London, 1972), 273. Lists of graduates in AU *Calendars* for 1932–3, 1937–8, 1942–3. For the abolition of the degree, Court Minutes, 8 June, 13 December 1949.
4 Segal Quince Wicksteed, *Review of the Financial Situation and Prospects of the University of Aberdeen* (UGC, 1988), 2.6. cf above, pp 12–13.
5 R S Moore, 'Sociologists not at work', in G Littlejohn, ed., *Power and the State* (London, 1978).
6 Penny Griffin, ed., *One Hundred Years of Women's Education in Oxford* (London, 1986), 179, 199, 201.
7 *Robbins Report*, 6–7.

Appendix

Some Statistical Tables, 1945–1981

TABLE 1   STUDENT NUMBERS

	1945–6	1950–1	1955–6	1960–1	1965–6	1970–1	1975–6	1980–1
a) UNDERGRADUATES								
Total	1278	1790	1615	1903	3469	4943	4534	4769
Men	763	1285	1121	1283	2187	3054	2668	2578
Women	515	505	494	620	1282	1889	1866	2191
Arts	457	713	649	842	1695+94 BEd	2408+292	1929+277	1916+147
Science	324	498	482	591	1100	1672	1658	1740
Divinity	14	30	15	4	18	40	39	63
Law	25	45	42	41	126	212	360	442
Medicine	458	504	427	425	530	611	548	608
b) POSTGRADUATES								
Full-time Research	16	63	77	105	215	337	328	339
Full-time Courses (not shown separately until 1972–3)							118	97
Doctorates awarded	10	24	33	29	40	63	54	73
P/G Masters	—	—	—	5	28	59	106	109
Diplomas & Certificates	1	11	29	23	38	76	108	104
c) OVERSEAS STUDENTS (FT)	41	55	114	216 (inc. P.T)	231	171	381	399
d) STUDENTS IN HALLS OF RESIDENCE	35	—	19	141	195	1293	1973	2830

SOURCE: Annual Statistical Returns, consulted in University Registry.

NOTE: There are certain difficulties in establishing comparable figures, due to changes in classifying, for example, candidates for the former EdB degree (included here as undergraduates in the faculty of arts). Candidates for the MEd degree which replaced it in 1965 are not included in this table; they appear in the returns among 'other postgraduates'.

We have illustrated the growth in this heterogeneous group by figures of postgraduate awards rather than series of student numbers. In 1980–1 the full postgraduate total was 773, comprising 339 full-time and 139 part-time research students; 97 full-time and 7 part-time students on postgraduate courses; 28 candidates for the Dip Ed, 17 for the MEd, 45 for the Certificate in Advanced Social Studies, 12 for the Certificate in Accountancy Studies, 58 for the Diploma in Legal Practice, 7 for the Diploma in Medical Radio-Diagnosis; and 24 others.

TABLE 2 HOME ADDRESSES OF FULL-TIME STUDENTS (Undergraduates and Postgraduates)

	1945–6	1950–1	1955–6		1960–1★	1965–6	1970–1		1975–6	1980–1
Within 30 miles of Aberdeen	756 (56%)	1062 (54.3%)	836 (49%)	Aberdeenshire	1156 (51%)	1549 (41%)	2107 (39%)	Aberdeen City	1224 (21.6%)	1023 (17.75%)
				Banff / Moray / Highlands & Islands / Kincardine / Angus	581 (25.7%)	861 (22.8%)	1272 (23.5%)	Other Grampian	1152 (20.4%)	927 (16%)
								Highlands & Islands	534 (9.4%)	483 (8.3%)
Other U.K.	550 (40%)	839 (42.9%)	756 (44.2%)	Other Scotland	111 (5%)	432 (11.5%)	1086 (20%)	Other Scotland	1742 (30.7%)	2032 (35.2%)
				England, Wales & N. Ireland	195 (8.6%)	692 (18.3%)	757 (14%)		629 (11%)	895 (15.9%)
Overseas	41 (3%)	55 (2.8%)	114 (6.8%)	Overseas	216 (9.6%)	231 (6.1%)	171 (3.2%)		381 (6.7%)	399 (6.9%)
	1347	1956	1706		2259	3765	5393		5662	5759

★ 1960–1 figures include part-time students.

TABLE 3 STAFF AND UNIVERSITY GOVERNMENT

	1945-6	1950-1	1955-6	1960-1	1965-6	1970-1	1975-6	1980-1
a) STAFF (Women in brackets)								
Professors	29 (—)	36 (—)	38 (—)	40 (—)	53 (1=1.8%)	63 (1=1.58%)	76 (2=2.63%)	78 (1=1.2%)
Other Full-time Academics	87 (14=16%)	191 (19=9.9%)	248 (29=11.6%)	287 (16=5.5%)	441 (42=9.5%)	559 (48=8.5%)	651 (53=8.1%)	677 (60=8.8%)
Part-time	61 (7=11.4%)	75 (9=12%)	75 (6=8%)	86 (7=8.1%)	148 (13=8.7%)	89 (17=19.1%)	317 (38=11.9%)	473 (63=13.3%)
Research	2 (1=50%)	11 (5=45.4%)	11 (2=18.1%)	42 (12=28.5%)	79 (32=40.5%)	152 (46=30.2%)	185 (60=32.4%)	242 (92=38%)
Office	2	3	7 (1=14.2%)	10 (1=10%)	30 (8=26.6%)	51 (16=31.3%)	59 (24=40.6%)	65 (28=43%)
Library	2 (—)	2 (—)	2 (—)	8 (5=62.5%)	20 (10=50%)	21 (9=42.8%)	31 (19=61.2%)	34 (20=58.8%)
Computing Services	— (—)	— (—)	— (—)	—	2 (—)	12 (1=8.3%)	21 (1=4.76%)	28 (9=32.1%)
b) UNIVERSITY GOVERNMENT (Women in brackets)								
Membership of Court	14 (—)	14 (1)	14 (1)	14 (1)	14 (1)	17 (2)	18 (1)	21 (3)
Membership of Senatus	33 (—)	44 (—)	46 (—)	49 (—)	63 (1)	93 (2)	136 (6)	149 (8)

SOURCE: Court Minutes, University Calendars.
NOTE: Figures for Office, Library & Computing Services, which show senior staff, have not been moderated to allow for changes in grading. Numbers of other staff do not seem to have been recorded earlier than 1973; even after that they exclude manual staff.

T_{ABLE} 4 Sources of University Income (Current Prices)

	1945–6	1950–1	1955–6	1960–1	1965–6	1970–1	1975–6	1980–1
University Income	£211,174	£541,978	£763,150	£1,263,429	£3,156,504	£6,044,661	£14,253,344	£30,656,988
Parliamentary/ UGC Grants	110,721 (52%)	392,640 (72.4%)	586,310 (76.8%)	1,002,864 (79.3%)	2,371,359 (75%)	4,420,315 (73%)	11,140,348 (78%)	20,414,200 (66.5%)
Fees	48,456 (22.9%)	71,978 (13.2%)	64,999 (8.5%)	102,929 (8.1%)	295,575 (9.3%)	422,875 (7%)	811,769 (5.7%)	4,640,849 (15%)
Endowments	26,036 (12.3%)	27,103 (5%)	30,408 (4%)	38,193 (3%)	39,787 (1.2%)	57,864 (1%)	76,575 (0.5%)	197,326 (0.6%)
Grants for Research	[2,656★] (1.25%)	[19,754★] (3.6%)	[20,533★] (2.7%)	50,925 (4%)	252,617 (8%)	511,195 (8.5%)	976,679 (6.8%)	2,581,834 (8.4%)

★ Figures for 'Donations and Subscriptions'. In 1961 £33,244 (83%) of the previous year's total of £40,016 was reallocated to 'Research'.
SOURCE: University Accounts.

TABLE 5 THE ESTABLISHMENT OF NEW DEPARTMENTS IN ABERDEEN UNIVERSITY 1945–81

This table summarises the creation and expansion of academic departments in the University of Aberdeen. Each point on the line represents one year within the period 1945–81. C.... indicates a department with one established chair in the year in question; 2C::: indicates two (or in some cases more) chairs. (Chairs which were never filled are not included.) R indicates a department headed by a reader; P, by a personal professor; L, by a lecturer or senior lecturer; p indicates a part-time appointment; + indicates departments closed or threatened with closure 1981–8.

FACULTY OF ARTS [and SOCIAL SCIENCE, 1975]

Department	L date	C date	Line	
Humanity		C 1505	C C	} Clas +
Greek		C 1505	C C	} Clas
Moral Phil		C 1505	C C	} Phil
Logic		C 1505	C C	} Phil
Maths		C 1505	C ....2C......................... C	
English		C 1893	C ....2C..................... C	
French		C 1926	C ....2C................... C	
Psychology	L1893		RC ....2C..................	
History	L1896	C 1903	C ....2C..........3C.............	
Education	L1898		LLRRRRRRRRRRRRRRRRC	+
German	L1898		LLRRRC	
Statistics	L1903		LLLLLLLLRRRRRRRRRC	
Celtic	L1906		RRRRRRRRRRRRRRRRRRRRRRRRRRLLLLLLLLLLLL	
Geography	L1916		RRRRRRC ....2C....................	
Spanish	L1916		LLLRRRRLLLLLLLLLLLLRRRRRRRRRRRRRRRLLLL	
Pol Econ	L1902	C 1921	C ....2C.... LLLRRRRRLLLLLLLLLLLLLLRRRRRRRRRRRLLLL	
Ec Hist	L1923		C ... LLLLLLLLLLLLLLLLLLLLLLLLRRC	
Rel/Bib Studies	L1945		LLLLLLLLLLLLLLLLLLLLLLLLLLLLLLLLLRRRPPP	+
Music	L(p)1925		pLLLRRRRRRRLLLLLLLLLLLLLRRRRRRRRRRRRRR	+
Politics			LLLLLLLLLLLLLLLLLC	
Inter Rel			LLLLLLLLLLLLLLLLLLLLLLLLLLLLLLLLLLLLC	
Swedish			LLLLLLLLLLLLLLLLLLLLLLLLLLLLLLLLLLLLLLRR	+
Italian			LLLLLLLLLLLLLLLLLLLLLLLLLLLLLLLLLLLLLLLL	+

Accountancy		LLLLLLLLLLLC	
Computing		LLLLLLLLLLLLLLLLLLLLL	
Sociology		C . . . . . 2C : : : : : : : :	+
Med Sociology		C	+
Russian		LLLLLLLRRRRRRRR	
History of Art		LLLLLLLRRR	
Social Work		C	+
Linguistics		LLLLLLLL	+
ISSPA		C	+

FACULTY OF DIVINITY

Church History	Chair 1616	C . . . .
Sys Theology	Chair 1620	C . . . .
Christian Dogmatics	Chair 1934	C . . . . }
Hebrew	Chair 1673	C . . . . {
Bib Crit [N.T.]	Chair 1616	C . . . .
Practical Theology	Chair 1934	CCCppppppppppppppppppppppppppppppp

FACULTY OF LAW

[Private] Law	Chair 1505	C . . . .
Conveyancing	Ch(p) 1927	ppppppppppppppppppppppppppppppC . . .
Jurisprudence		C . . . .
Public Law		LLLLLLLLLLLLLLLC . . . .
Land Economy		C . . . .

FACULTY OF SCIENCE

Nat Phil	Chair 1505	C . . . .
Nat History	Chair 1593	C . . . . 2C : : :
Chemistry	Chair 1793	C . . . . 2 3C : : : : : :
Botany	Chair 1860	C . . . . 4C : : : : : :
Agriculture	Chair 1911	C . . . . 2C : : : : : :
Ag Econ		LLLLLLLLLLLLLLC . . . . . . +
Animal Prod		C . . . . : : : :

FACULTY OF SCIENCE—*continued*

Geology	Chair 1922	C . . . . 2C . . . . .
Engineering	Chair 1923	C . . . . 2C . . . .
Forestry	Chair 1626	C . . . .
Bio-Chemistry		C . . . .
Soil Science		L L L L L L L R R R R R R R R R R R R R C . . . . . .
H P S		L L L R R R R R R R R R R R R R L L L L L L L L L L L
Genetics		C . . . . +
Dev Biology		R R R R R R R R R R R R R R R R
Microbiology		L L R R R R R R R R P

FACULTY OF MEDICINE

Medicine	Chair 1505	C . . . .
Surgery	Chair 1839	C . . . .
Anatomy	Chair 1839	C . . . .
Obstetrics	Chair 1860	C . . . .
Physiology	Chair 1860	C . . . .
Therapeutics	Chair 1860	C . . . .
Pathology	Chair 1882	C . . . .
Bacteriology	Chair 1920	C . . . .
Mental Health		C . . . . .
Child Health		C . . . .
Social Medicine		C . . . .
Chem Pathology		C . . .
Med Physics		C . .
Gen Practice		R R R C . .
Pharmacology		C . .